OUT THERE

a camper cookbook

RECIPES FROM THE WILD

Lee Kalpakis

Photography by Brittany Barb

weldon**owen**

For Jeff, Tim, Mom & Dad, for a lifetime
of support and inspiration.

And for Sean and Mac, without whom
none of this would be possible.

contents

Open-Fire Projects

Backpack Food

Canteen Cocktails

Salad Stuff

Easy Sweets

back to the mountains

John Burroughs, one of my favorite writers, was a famous naturalist born in the Catskills and known for his deep connection to the natural world. He wrote, "The most precious things of life are near at hand, without money and without price. Each of you has the whole wealth of the universe at your very door. All that I ever had, and still have, may be yours by stretching forth your hand and taking it." And when I read that, boy, did it stick with me.

My name is Lee Kalpakis and I live in a twenty-two-foot-long 1976 Fleetwood Prowler camper in the woods of the Catskill Mountains. I am also a professional cook. It would have been easy, when I set out on this adventure, opting for an alternative lifestyle, to rely on peanut-butter-and-jelly sandwiches and canned soup. But daydreaming about exciting meals and looking forward to making them has kept me at my happiest here and has opened up an entirely new world for me.

I feel that I'm exactly where I should be, that I've been barreling toward living this way for a long time. I felt a calling to live like this before I understood what it would mean. And although some days I'm still frazzled with anxiety living this way—away from people in a tiny makeshift home nestled among the trees—overall it has felt like medicine. Cooking in this small, unconventional space has been a challenge to be enjoyed—one that leaves me with more understanding every time I fail. And teaching myself to extend my kitchen to the outdoors has been the most exciting part. If I've learned anything through cooking in and around this little camper, it's that leaning into simplicity is what helps replace frustration with joy.

It's not an easy way to live. A lot of the time it feels like a fight with nature instead of living in harmony with it, which is the intention. In the past year and a half, Sean, my partner of ten years; our dog, Mac; and I have experienced flooding, rodent infestation (mice yes, but also an occasional chipmunk on the kitchen counter), hornet stings, Lyme disease (yep, all three of us), frozen pipes, blizzards, bears, fallen trees, and a giant feral pig. But we continue to stay. Waking up in a camper we renovated with our own hands, stepping out into the morning amid old trees and shafts of sunlight, and starting a fire for breakfast make everything worth it. It is messy, difficult, and exhausting, but it's still so worth it.

I should mention that this isn't our permanent residence. We created this temporary home to live in while we build our first real home—a small and simple cabin, also surrounded by trees. I also should mention that, before this, I had absolutely no carpentry experience. It has been an overwhelming couple of years, one filled with unimaginable highs and crushing lows. But this time has also been the kind that makes you feel alive, like you aren't just coasting through life. And above all the feelings—good and bad—most of all I'm just looking to feel alive and present.

In years before this, I experienced the discomfort of being stagnant, of a life consumed by a job you hate. Waking up every day wishing it was already over, desperately wanting to be somewhere else far away, going through the hollow motions of daydreaming about some other chapter of my life that hopefully would come one day. And I only got myself out of that headspace and into the chapter I'd hoped for by saying yes to a poorly planned wild idea and, for the first time since I was a kid, truly stepping outside again.

I was born and raised in New York's Hudson Valley. I've said that so many times that I am sick of hearing myself repeat it. But it is true, and it's a gigantic part of who I am. When I was a kid, I lived in a dreamland. I grew up in the hamlet of Olivebridge, in a house that was brought up from the valley that was flooded to create the Ashokan Reservoir. Our home was surrounded by meadows, forest, a pond, mountain views, and a horse farm across the street. It wasn't anything fancy but to me it was paradise. Every day that I wasn't in school or busy with some extracurricular activity, I'd set out to do my favorite thing in the world: play outside. It felt like meditation, though I don't think I knew what meditation was yet. I'd stare at fields, climb trees, taste the tree sap that stained my fingers. I'd fish the pond, turning large rocks over looking for the chubbiest worms to use as bait. I'd climb to the top of the hill in our back field, stand there, listen to the wind, and think about how it felt on my skin. I'd lie down on the ground and watch the treetops move. I'd smell lilacs and pick iris, and I'd eat strawberries

from under the largest catalpa tree. I'd stuff my mouth with pineapple mint and drink from the hose, making a fun little beverage in my mouth. I'd talk to spiders, check on birds' nests, and sing to myself. This was my happiest time. I didn't really want to go inside to watch TV, didn't want friends to come over, didn't want to do much of anything but observe what was happening outside.

Our family's restaurant was also brought up from the reservoir site. Steeped in local history, Winchell's sat just across the water from Olivebridge in the town of Shokan. Working there with my dad was my first job. Both my big brothers worked there, too. Within the building, next to the restaurant, we also had an antique store where you could usually find my mom selling furniture to wealthy tourists from the city.

Winchell's was at the center of all our lives. It was who we were as a family for many years. I first fell in love with cooking while working the early shift with my dad during my summer breaks from school. I'd watch him bake bread, make soups from scratch, and toss pizza dough high over his head. I worked the counter, served tables, and helped him prep things for dinner service like meatballs and chocolate chip cookies. We'd work on projects like frozen custard flavors and lunch specials while listening to Van Morrison and Levon Helm. I loved the quiet focus of chopping vegetables and rolling out pizza dough.

Then I turned eighteen and life felt different. I didn't make time for going outside and I lost interest in the restaurant. It was a rush of pressure and emotion, of social engagements and expectations—an introduction to true stress that felt exciting. Friends, "lovers,"

partying, lots and lots of partying. This rush continued all through my twenties. I chose to go to the city for college and stayed there for years after. Connecting or maybe disconnecting. Pushing myself, finding myself, working myself to exhaustion, getting my heart broken, really, really broken, feeling my world cave in. Moving and pushing and struggling, wanting but not really knowing exactly what. Coming back up to the Hudson Valley felt like waking up from a fever dream. For the first time in over a decade, everything slowed down. But the dream wasn't for nothing. I woke up with skills and passion, a loving partner to share my life with, and a diligent work ethic I was proud of. Living in that city world made me stronger and smarter—and eager to return to what I missed. I was ready to go back home.

the camper

Before the COVID-19 pandemic, Sean got a car and we started spending weekends upstate. Before we knew it, we were spending every weekend upstate. When the lockdown happened, we stayed at his dad's house for what we thought would be two weeks, and we never moved back to Brooklyn. We made a plan—and acted fast—to build a home and live in a camper while we worked. The very last night we spent in our Bushwick loft was the Fourth of July. I remember looking out our giant wall of windows and seeing fireworks all across the skyline. I turned to Sean, who was staring at his phone, as he said, "I found it" and showed me a photo of a vintage camper. It had a retro yellow-and-orange stripe and looked like the mini version of the one in *The Long, Long Trailer* starring Lucille Ball and Desi Arnaz. It was what we had been looking for. The next morning, we left the city bright and early for Roxbury, New York, which happens to be where John Burroughs was born and raised, to get the camper in exchange for $1,500. Driving past my parents' old restaurant, out west on Route 28, through endless farmland met by soft, low foothills, we met a man who lived up a horribly rough dirt road, much like the one we would later live on. He was kind and easy to talk to. He towed the camper to Sean's dad's property for us, where it lived for a long time. We renovated the camper there, working day and night in the intense summer heat.

When September came and the air started to cool, we moved the camper to the plot of land we had bought for cheap up in the mountains and spent the first of many, many nights there. If I remember correctly, I made a pasta dish with sausage, peppers, and acorn squash over the fire. For the next morning with coffee, I made golden tomato sandwiches with garlicky yogurt and lots of olive oil. The process of making both meals was messy, but it was what I had long been dreaming about. Adjusting to life in the camper was messy too. But again, it was what I'd

been hoping for. I found the silence of the woods at night unsettling; so did Mac. Every time a twig would snap at night, Mac would bark and howl, which didn't make things easier for me. He and I would feed off each other's anxieties while Sean slept peacefully beside us. As time went on, things got easier. I began to love the quiet and look forward to the owl sounds at night. I think we're fed the idea that nighttime in the woods is dangerous, but once you realize that there's nothing out there that's out to get you, you sleep peacefully.

Winter came and things didn't feel as dreamy anymore. We were hit with a monstrous season: several feet of snow, ice, wind, even flooding. Our little heater and tiny wood stove kept us warm enough, but we had to wear sweaters and hats to bed most nights. Sean encouraged me to deal with it all by getting outside to snowboard with him, which helped at times. But mostly I stayed in to cook. I went from feeling trapped to feeling cozied up every time I planned a meal. I focused on practicing cooking in my new, strange, little space, and I started to understand how to make the camper work for me. I was simmering stock and soup, roasting chickens, and making potpies just like I used to. I was proving to myself that I was able to cook pretty much whatever I wanted to comfort me during the hardest winter of my life.

Then the ice melted and the snow was gone. The sweaters and hats came off, and we were able to step outside. That's when the outdoor cooking really shifted. I abandoned the gas grill and obsessed over charcoal and wood. Sean built an open smoking rig, and I practiced my fire building. For long periods of time, we exclusively cooked on a campfire. Our clothes smelled like smoke when we went to bed, and my hair smelled like it even after I'd washed it. Our fingernails were always dirty, but we were happy and full and always excited for the next big cook.

the cabin

Sean is a carpenter—a very good one too. At some point we made the decision to build our first house all on our own: another pretty extreme challenge. For a while, we just enjoyed living in the woods while we planned. Sean made the architectural drawings as we dreamed up the best living space given what we could afford. During that time, we indulged in the bliss of summertime in the Catskills. We filled out mountains of paperwork and waited for permits and approvals and researched for hours. Yet we still found time to swim in our favorite creeks, climb to our favorite peaks, watch the sunset, and enjoy a fire every evening.

Once it was time to actually start building, I felt a rude awakening from an idyllic summer dream. We were racing against the cold to finish the foundation. Day after day after day, we were working in the dirt, taking pickaxes to giant boulders in the ground. The excavation, the plumbing, the concrete pour. I felt so proud of Sean and so grateful to our community for helping wherever they could. But I was completely overwhelmed and exhausted by it all. We stood our walls up—just the two of us—in fifteen-degree weather. We built the roof—just the two of us—with a foot of snow on the ground.

During that time, we couldn't stay in the camper full-time. A long, hot shower at the end of the day was the only thing keeping me from fully giving up. So we spent some time at Sean's dad's house in Hurley and at our sweet friends' weekend home in Hudson. I am so grateful for that time, and although at first I felt defeated, in retrospect, it's what we needed. I remind myself that even Henry David Thoreau did laundry at his mom's house while writing *Walden*. We all need a little help sometimes. Instead of feeling like a failure for asking for help, I feel lucky for having the option to ask and having people in our lives willing to lend a hand.

Now I sit here, on the couch, in our cabin. It is not yet finished, but it is already extraordinary. It has a working shower, it is warm, and the way the light pours in through the giant windows is unreal. I'll be happy if we never have to carry roof beams up a hill in a snowstorm again, but I can look back on the experience with pride. I smile now, knowing that when this book comes out and as you're reading this, Sean, Mac, and I will be settled in our home that we built ourselves from the ground up. I'm slowly coming to feel a deep sense of accomplishment that I've never known before.

living in the woods

One freezing-cold night as we were falling asleep, we heard a loud shriek. The sound was sharp and continuous, like a little yapping dog crossed with a crying child. It was terrifying to me—terrifying because it was unknown. We heard the sound quickly move from the south end of our property to the north end. I remember my heart racing and the hair on the back of my neck standing up. The fear of the unknown. I jumped up to research what the sound was. Growing up in Olivebridge, I'd never heard that animal. Maybe it wasn't an animal? Maybe the "woods witch" I had had a dream about was real? After a quick Google search, Sean and I found a website that played recordings of every native species in the Catskills and discovered it had been a red fox. My fear was quickly replaced with overwhelming excitement. A beautiful red fox so close—gracing us with its presence. I felt so lucky to hear it.

That quick turnaround made a big impact on me. I realized that it was the unknown that scared me, not the woods. Knowing makes the fear go away. That kind of understanding made me want to learn everything about my surroundings. I began to look forward to the nighttime sounds—to hearing two owls calling to each other and eventually getting together to hang out, the howling of coyotes, the quiet steps of a black bear roaming the property. I even saw a fisher just this morning! Instead of resisting it, I'm now marveling at the wildlife around me. Nothing is here to harm me. All the creatures were here long before we were. It's been the greatest joy to learn about them and how to live symbiotically with them, to truly enjoy their nearness. Recently I read John Burroughs's "The Snow-Walkers," an essay about winter in the Catskills. In it he wrote the following:

> I see the hills, bulging with great drifts, lift themselves up cold and white against the sky, the black lines of fences here and there obliterated by the depth of the snow. Presently a fox barks away up the next mountain, and I imagine I can almost see him sitting there, in his furs, upon the illuminated surface, and looking down in my direction. As I listen, one answers him from behind the woods in the valley. What a wild winter sound, wild and weird, up among the ghostly hills! Since the wolf has ceased to howl upon these mountains, and the panther to scream, there is nothing to be compared with it. So wild! I get up in the middle of the night to hear it. It is refreshing to the ear, and one delights to know that such wild creatures are among us.

When I read that I realized that although living decades apart, Burroughs and I had a shared experience. My growing gratitude for the wild and weird of my surroundings felt so right.

ABOUT THIS BOOK

Whether you're living in a camper or just camping for the weekend, I want this book to be a guide to simplify your operation and encourage you to think outside the hot dog and s'more box. There is a wonderful middle ground between committing to using fewer ingredients and exploring possibilities. I hope this book will teach habits that will stick with you while inspiring you to be creative in the process.

It's hard enough to follow a recipe to the letter in a conventional cooking space, so I'll never ask you to be rigid in following a recipe out in the wild. Sometimes the market or farm stand won't have what a recipe calls for. Sometimes you're headed to the woods for the weekend and forgot an ingredient at home. Sometimes the only place for groceries is a gas station. This lifestyle is about making do, and I see that as a gift. I believe that one of the greatest skills a good cook can have is knowing how to properly swap ingredients. It can even make the meal feel more rewarding. With any of these recipes, it's important, first and foremost, to enjoy yourself and ultimately just to do your best. Swap cilantro for basil, use Kalamata instead of Castelvetrano olives, and I'm sure rye bread will be just as delicious as sourdough. All the recipes in this book are based on what's easily available to me here in upstate New York, and that availability looks different to all of us. All you have to do is let the ingredients you *can* get your hands on guide you.

I also want these recipes to serve as a way to get more out of your campfire experience. Maybe you're camping for a few days, maybe you're staying in a tiny home for vacation, or maybe you live in a yurt or a trailer or an RV. Maybe you're traveling cross-country in a Sprinter van, or maybe you're backpacking and sleeping in a tent. Whatever your adventure, you can use these recipes however you want. Follow them exactly, substitute ingredients as you wish, or just use the photos as inspiration. My goal is to show how fun cooking outdoors or in an alternative living space can be. Giving up mainstream luxuries does the human brain and body good, and it doesn't mean you have to eat granola for every meal. Celebrating food while living this way is exhilarating. The joy you feel surrounded by nature and during an incredible meal should be experienced together. It was meant to be!

OUTFITTING
A TINY KITCHEN

During our time in Bushwick, I worked as a recipe developer, cooking-show host, culinary producer, food stylist, and private chef, so I had accumulated a serious kitchen collection in the years leading up to our transition back upstate. When we moved to the camper, I had boxes and boxes of cooking tools and appliances. I kept everything in our shed and took things out as needed. Several months into living there, most of the boxes in the shed were still full, which made me realize that what I considered essential was a very short list—much shorter than expected. Here is my list of must-have tools for a small kitchen.

essential tools

Cooler. A large, high-quality cooler is a necessity. We are so pleased with our YETI. Expensive, yes, but worth it.

Chef's knife. If I had to pick just one knife to have with me in the woods, a chef's knife would be it. It is great for doing everything from chopping herbs to dicing an onion to carving a chicken.

Paring knife. Essentially a shorter version of a chef's knife, a paring knife is useful for such tasks as cutting citrus and peeling apples. I also sometimes wrap mine in a napkin and take it with me on a picnic for slicing cheese.

Serrated knife. A wonderful option to have around for slicing bread. Most of the loaves at my local farm stand aren't sliced, and it's nice to be able to cut bread easily.

Knife roll and knife magnet. Keep your knives somewhere safe. Shoving them into a drawer causes them to dull from rubbing up against one another, and knife blocks are unhygienic and take up way too much space. I love keeping my knives on a magnet.

Two cutting boards. One wooden and one plastic. I use a smaller plastic one for raw meat and fish and a larger wooden one for everything else. I also sometimes use them as serving platters.

12-inch cast-iron frying pan. I use mine on the campfire, inside the camper, and for almost every meal. It's the most important pan I own. I have a few antique ones I've used over the years, but I love my Lodge cast-iron frying pan the most. It's my old faithful—the one I just keep going back to. It's reliable and easy, and if I leave it out in the rain, it's a quick fix to restore it. I recommend picking just one cast-iron pan and using it frequently so you really break it in. Season it well, and after a while, it becomes an extension of you. If you are able to find a cast-iron pan with a lid, you've hit the jackpot because they're hard to find. I use the cast-iron lid from my Lodge camp Dutch oven on my frying pan. Both are 12-inch so the lid works interchangeably, which comes in handy when you want to trap heat above what you're cooking. For example: a sunny-side-up egg or cheese over a burger.

Cast-iron Dutch oven. I use my 5½-quart enameled cast-iron Le Creuset Dutch oven almost as much as my cast-iron frying pan. I've been using it for many years, and when I started really cooking over fire, I was hesitant to bring it outside. But I'm glad I did. I try to be mindful of the flame when I'm using it, as I don't want to blacken the sides too much. But to be honest, the soot comes off pretty easily, and I've found my Le Creuset stands up to some seriously raging fires. I also have a 6-quart cast-iron Dutch oven, which is a whole other animal. It's less precious and feels more like an oven than a pot. I nestle it right in the hottest embers and throw hot coals onto the lid. It has the ability to cook whatever you are making from all sides, which is incredibly useful.

Baking pan. I have a square pan for things like brownies and jam bars and a round pie pan too, but having just one will serve you well. Mine are small enough—just 9 × 9 inches with 1½- to 2-inch sides—to fit into my tiny little oven, and they bake whatever I need. No muffin pan, no Bundt pan, nothing fancy at all. Any muffin recipe will do just fine as a cake. Even a cookie recipe is more fun as one giant cookie to slice. A camper is not the place for fussy baking.

Baking dish. I keep a small oval baking dish in the camper for desserts like crisps and cobblers. I also use it for roasting things like chicken and vegetables.

Saucepan. Small or medium. This comes in handy when melting butter to bake with, it works well for heating up a single portion of leftovers, I make jam out of overripe fruit in it, and it is most often used in our home for making a speedy package of ramen noodles.

Quarter sheet pans. These 9 × 13-inch pans with 1-inch sides are for roasting and toasting but mostly for prepping. There's something soothing about your *mise en place* fitting perfectly on a quarter sheet pan.

Wire racks. Purchasing a wire rack for each sheet pan is helpful. If you need something to stay crispy as it cools or you want to drain off the excess oil from items just fried, a wire rack is a must. Wire racks are used in professional kitchens, save paper towels, and are less messy. Look for wire racks sized to fit your quarter sheet pans.

Nesting mixing bowls. If I could manage with just one bowl, I would, but it's not realistic. For the amount of cooking I do in the camper, I need large, medium, and small mixing bowls. Anything that nests is a camper's best friend.

Tongs. You need both big and little ones! The big guys are for grilling and the little ones are for tossing salads, sautéing, serving pastas, and more.

Wooden spoon. A true necessity—and an obvious one. I feel like my entire identity as a recipe developer is based on deglazing a pan, and nothing gets the job done like a wooden spoon.

Pastry brush. Essential for any sort of barbecuing.

Fish spatula. My favorite spatula—so thin and perfectly shaped. It is able to handle the most delicate fish, fritter, or pancake with grace and respect. And I use it every time I sear a piece of meat. With a fish spatula, a wooden spoon, and a rubber spatula on hand, I don't see a need for a regular metal or plastic spatula at all.

Rubber spatula. This indispensable tool ensures there is little to no waste when baking. I actually tried to do without one when we first moved into the camper. But every time I baked something, I'd be frustrated by the amount of batter left in the bowl. A rubber spatula is crucial to getting every last drop, and it makes dishwashing easier too.

Vegetable peeler. Another tool I tried to do without for a while. I thought, "I have a paring knife, so I don't need a peeler in the camper." But boy, did I miss it. The peeler just gets things done faster.

Box grater. I've always been a Microplane girl, but in the camper, I discovered the box grater to be more versatile. I like that I can use it to grate lemon zest, garlic, and ginger and still have the option to grate soft cheeses, carrots, or onions.

Instant-read thermometer. Grilling meat can be intimidating because there's a lot at stake. A thermometer is especially important when you're cooking outside, as the time of year and temperature can lead to dramatic changes in the outcome of a recipe. So why not take the guesswork out of it? A good instant-read thermometer will let you know exactly when your meat should be pulled from the heat.

Oven thermometer. But if you do happen to have a camper oven or you're just using this book to cook in your regular kitchen, the built-in oven thermostat is often inaccurate. An oven thermometer will allow you to set the oven dial to the correct temperature for a recipe and to monitor the temperature during the cooking process.

Immersion blender. I wanted this book to be as stripped down as possible. I wanted to illustrate how much you can do with just fire, some oil, and a knife. But the truth is, things aren't always that romantic when you're actually in the thick of living in such a tiny space. Of all the things I missed about a typical living space, my Vitamix blender was right up there with long showers and air-conditioning. But bringing that big thing to the camper and lugging it over to our generator for a morning smoothie felt, um, foolish, so I purchased my first immersion blender. It was something I had enjoyed using at work but always sort of scoffed at because a stand blender seemed more useful at home. Although it didn't seem useful enough to have my own back then, in a tiny camper kitchen, I find myself reaching for the immersion blender again and again.

Kitchen towels. A mess in the camper feels ten times bigger than a mess in a regular kitchen. I have a stack of towels for spills and general tidying up. I also use them for wrapping utensils for packed food, I drape them over dough that is proofing, I wrap tortillas in them to keep warm, and I lay lettuces on them to dry after washing. I try to avoid unnecessary paper towel use, but I do keep a roll under the sink for things like patting meat dry before seasoning.

Parchment paper. This may not be a necessity for you, but it is for me. Cooking in a camper is just one big game of "How can I dirty the least number of dishes?" A bit of parchment helps me. I bake, roast, and toast with a parchment paper–lined pan to avoid a mess. I also try to use each piece multiple times, then usually toss it into the fire once it's on its last leg.

Aluminum foil. I use foil for storing leftovers and trapping heat over a pan in lieu of a lid.

pantry essentials

Kosher salt. I use Diamond Crystal kosher salt. It's light and fluffy and mellow, so there's less risk of oversalting than when using other kosher salts. I like sea salt or pink salt just fine, but I prefer always to use the same brand so I know exactly how much I need.

Flaky salt. Maldon. Always. Nothing pulls you out of the funk from a hard day of living in the wilderness like topping off your bowl of beans with fancy finishing salt.

Black pepper. Get a pepper mill and grind it fresh for full-flavored cracked black pepper!

Spices. This varies, but the spices I typically have on hand are smoked paprika, ground cumin, onion powder, ground cardamom, ground cinnamon, fennel seeds, and ground sumac. I'd say pick your favorites and keep the number under ten.

Vinegar. If you taste a dish you're working on and it seems flat or imbalanced, a splash of vinegar is usually the solution. It's essential in my camper kitchen as well as every other kind of kitchen there is!

Soy sauce or tamari. For seasoning salads, soups, and grains and for marinating meat. Look for a brand that is naturally (or traditionally) brewed for the best flavor.

Pasta. It's fun to have pasta on hand to plan out a delicious and indulgent dinner, but to be honest, we use it mostly at the end of a long day, when we're starving and need something quick. It's a necessity because it takes no time at all to make.

Tinned fish. A wonderful quick fix when you're hungry in a camper. My pantry is stacked with beautiful little tins of mussels, oysters, mackerel, sardines, and trout. I love them all on toast or in a salad. They're great marinated in a quick citrusy dressing or straight out of the tin.

All-purpose flour. For baking, for pancakes, for whatever, this is an obvious staple. I keep my bag of flour in a ziplock plastic bag for double protection against bugs, mice, and spillage.

Sugar. Mainly just for baking—oh and dry rubs! You'll find yourself using a pinch here and there for sauces and dressings too. You'll need both granulated sugar and brown sugar.

Baking powder. Indispensable for baking, both sweet and savory.

Baking soda. I keep one box in the pantry for baking and a tiny one in the mini fridge to keep it smelling fresh.

Sweet corn powder. I love this stuff. It's dehydrated corn ground into a fine powder. I add a couple of tablespoons to whatever I'm baking to make it taste like peak-season sweet corn. It works like magic. This is the only thing in my pantry that isn't sold at a grocery store. I buy it online and to me it's worth the extra effort. Maybe not quite an essential but most definitely a favorite.

perishable essentials

Lemons. The fruit I could never live without. It's hard to find a recipe in this book that doesn't include lemon.

Olive oil. I stock two olive oils: a basic one for cooking and a nice unfiltered extra-virgin for finishing. I like something intense and fruity for vinaigrettes and for drizzling.

Coconut oil. I use coconut oil for sautéing, baking, and for stews and soups. I also sometimes use it on my skin when I've run out of moisturizer.

Butter. I use European butter because of its high butterfat content. It makes for a richer flavor that's ideal for baking. I also love cultured butter, which has a sharper flavor compared to regular butter, making it perfect for things like garlic bread and butter-basted steak. I buy unsalted because I like to control how much salt goes into whatever I'm making.

Hot sauce. For obvious reasons. Mostly Cholula. Frank's Red Hot and sriracha too. Or anything from Poor Devil Pepper Co., a local favorite of ours. I try to only have one bottle of hot sauce at a time so as not to take up too much storage space, but it's a difficult rule to stick to.

Jarred anchovies. A favorite food and something I always have on hand. I melt them into sauces and butters and I think they make most salad dressings better. I also love them right out of the jar on a slice of good bread with butter. I buy the Ortiz anchovies that come in a glass jar instead of the canned kind. I find it easier to have a jar of them in the cooler or mini fridge. The idea of using only half a can of anchovies and figuring out how to store the rest in a camper kitchen is stressful to me.

Yogurt. One of my favorite condiments. Plain Greek yogurt flavored with grated raw garlic, lemon juice, salt, and olive oil is something I think goes with just about anything. Admittedly, as a Greek woman, I've been taught to use yogurt wherever I can.

Eggs. An obvious one. Found in most kitchens. But a slow morning in the camper isn't complete without a couple of eggs cracked into a pan of bubbling butter.

Buttermilk. You'll notice there are a number of recipes in this book that include buttermilk. It's because I never want to call for an ingredient that you'll use only a little bit of and then be left with, only to go bad. I love making buttermilk ranch dressing from scratch, but every time I've wanted to make it, I've had to buy a whole bottle and only use a few tablespoons. So I started incorporating buttermilk wherever I could to finish the bottle. It's fantastic in baking and can be used in so many ways. I've found it crucial to think that way to avoid any food waste. If I buy a bottle of buttermilk, it means I'm planning to make dressing, cake, and pancakes. Maybe I'll marinate some chicken thighs in it, and maybe I'll add some to a soup later in the week.

Parmesan cheese. The most versatile cheese. I shave and grate it over so many meals. I also believe that a leftover parmesan rind is the secret to making a soup or stew unforgettable.

Maple syrup. This is my go-to sweetener. I use sugar in baking and dry rubs but pure maple syrup for pretty much everything else: yogurt, oatmeal, smoothies, coffee, hot chocolate, and more.

on storage

Our kitchen has three tiny drawers and one shelf. There is absolutely no room for filler. The pantry, also tiny, is actually under our couch. That has always felt very smart and stealthy to me. We keep three tight-sealing plastic bins within the couch, and that makes a truly incredible space for dry goods and other nonperishables. The pantry is stocked differently as the seasons change, but mostly it's spices, flour, rice, pasta, canned beans and artichokes, tinned fish, snacks like crackers, popcorn kernels, extra bottles of oil, and emergency foods like Annie's mac and cheese and jars of tomato sauce. Our refrigerator is small and it's new. Most of the time we've spent in the camper has been completely off-grid, so we've relied on our YETI cooler for storing perishables. I'm grateful for every moment with this mini fridge and freezer. It has made our day-to-day life so much easier.

Think more dry goods and less perishable food in storage. Perishable food doesn't have the same shelf life in a cooler as it does in a refrigerator, so it's important to buy smaller amounts of produce, meat, and dairy while keeping a ton of nonperishable pantry staples on hand. This way you're able to come up with a meal that highlights the fresh stuff you have by supporting it with things like pasta, oatmeal, rice, nutritional yeast, quinoa, farro, barley, and beans. If the day gets away from you and you're left without any fresh produce or protein, some pasta, nutritional yeast, salt, pepper, and olive oil from your pantry will make a great meal. Stock your pantry wisely and you'll always have something to fall back on.

suggestions for easier cooking
and eating in a tiny space

Cook your pasta in the sauce. The truth is, with most pasta, slightly diluting the sauce and adding the dried pasta really works and makes the process much easier. You save on water and time, and you don't need to pull out an extra pot. It's not the way I do things in a typical kitchen but it just makes things a whole lot easier while camping.

Boil potatoes in batches that will last a few days. I can eat a potato at every meal. I never get bored. Ready-to-go boiled potatoes in our little fridge are at the center of my quick-meal world. When we've stayed out until dark and I need to throw something together because we're ravenous, when I need a little more to go with my eggs in the morning, or when I need a little late-night snack, a boiled potato always seems to be the answer. Ready in minutes if you fry them up in your cast-iron pan, perfect for turning random vegetables into a delicious hash, and even cold with a bit of salt, olive oil, and fresh herbs—they're quick, versatile, and always satisfying.

Cook grains and pasta in batches that will last a few days. This provides the same advantages as boiled potatoes but allows for even more variety. I love to keep cooked rice, pasta, quinoa, farro, and other grains on hand because throwing grains into a hot cast-iron pan with anything will make for an excellent dinner as long as there's salt and some kind of fat. Even just plain white rice fried in butter and sprinkled with salt can make for a comforting meal. Slide a little piece of medium-rare salmon on there with a drizzle of soy sauce, and it's a well-rounded experience.

Plant an herb garden. A bundle of herbs at the market may cost only a few dollars, but I use herbs so frequently that the dollars can really add up. And it's rare for me to use an entire bunch in one recipe, so occasionally I'm caught with a good amount of wilted herbs in my cooler. There are plenty of ways to incorporate droopy herbs into a wonderful meal, but I've found having live herbs around is much more efficient. Even if you're living in an RV or van and are constantly on the move, a little indoor herb garden can thrive near a window.

Designate a canteen for batch cocktails. Keeping a cocktail cold (or occasionally hot) is important. I've found that once anything other than water is stored in a canteen, it never really feels as pure as it once did. I've made the mistake of filling my trusty metal water bottle with wine, and as much as I scrub the inside clean, I can still smell the alcohol. So I have a designated canteen for my daily water and a separate one for mixing cocktails. That way, everything tastes as it should and stays at the perfect temperature.

Sour and salty make meals exciting. Olives, anchovies, capers, green peppercorns, sauerkraut, and cured meats will take up little room in your fridge yet pack plenty of punch and flavor. Sometimes after a long day of work, the farm stand is closed and a trip to the grocery store is out of the question. It's incredible what you can do with just a box of pasta and a couple of anchovies or a handful of crushed olives. It feels important to always have a bright and salty ingredient at hand. Bright flavors like these are a wonderful shortcut to a satisfying meal.

Keep your favorite condiments on hand. A good condiment can go a long way. Just as with sour and salty ingredients, we always keep our favorite condiments stocked to spice up something that might otherwise be boring. A top-notch hot sauce, a jar of chili crisp, Dijon mustard, barbecue sauce, and pesto—any of these has the power to make a grilled cheese or breakfast sandwich something special. While building our house, there were many days with the same old turkey sandwich for lunch. The right condiments on hand is a quick fix for a mundane meal.

Reimagine sweets. I've never had much of a sweet tooth, but I developed a pretty big one during the pandemic lockdown in 2020. So now, after dinner on most nights, I like to have a little something sweet. I've found the best form of dessert in the camper is, like everything else, something simple. Sometimes a few squares of chocolate will do the trick. Baking options are limited because of how old and nearly nonfunctional our oven is, but that doesn't mean we can't make something lovely for dessert. Instead of focusing on what I can't make because my oven doesn't bake things evenly, I've realized that there's a whole world of desserts that do just fine in my little 1970s setup. For example, a pavlova, soufflé, or angel food cake may not survive, but something more resilient to harsh flame and uneven heat distribution, such as a crisp or cobbler, comes out really well. So I lean into it—and honestly, those are my favorite kinds of desserts anyway. But maybe the most enjoyable dessert experience for me is actually somewhere between a few squares of chocolate and baking a cake.

I always keep a jar of jam, compote, or lemon curd in the cooler. At dessert time, I spoon a little onto a bowl of vanilla ice cream, yogurt, labneh, chia pudding, or even rice pudding. The result is an absolute delight.

Sandwiches are your best friends. As you make your way through this book, you may notice that I make a lot of sandwiches. I apologize to Brittany, my wonderful friend who photographed this book, because sandwiches are notoriously difficult to shoot. But with great patience, we managed to make them look beautiful. You'll find that while camping or living in a tiny home, a sandwich is the perfect meal. I'd confidently say that putting anything between two pieces of good bread makes it better, but it's not just pleasure I'm after. A sandwich is a sensible meal. It's your meal, your plate, and sometimes even your napkin. Portable, filling, and easy to put together, a sandwich is always going to be a campsite staple for me.

hosting in the wild

A lot of my happiness comes from solitude and stillness, but it also comes from sharing an experience with a group of buddies. Is it possible to have a "dinner party" while living in a little camper? I can tell you from experience, you absolutely can, and my goodness can it be fun. I try not to focus on matching plates or utensils or to dwell on how to make the dining space feel more like that of a typical home. Instead, I lean into the uniqueness. I try to remember my guests aren't there expecting a re-creation of their own home. They're visiting us out of curiosity and a desire to escape the ordinary. Most of all, I want to show them how incredible a meal can be out in the middle of the woods. Typically, I pull out a few sheet pans and fill them with handheld things like toasts, hot dogs, sandwiches, and dips. This way, our guests can sort of do as they please: fill a plate or just casually pop things straight from the pan into their mouths between sips of beer. Or I'll focus on one recipe in one large pot. Either way, it hardly makes any mess for me to clean up later on.

If your guests are up for it, make these meals a group activity. It's fun to sit around in the woods and drink beer with your buddies, but working together on dinner gets everyone involved and makes it a bonding experience. I love cooking with my friends. It's a great way to lean on one another and support one another at the same time. It always feels like a fun dance, and we're all learning one another's strengths in the choreography, whether it's gathering firewood, building the fire, or prepping the meal. If we all contribute in some way, sitting down to that meal feels like a team victory. We all played our part in this beautiful work of art that will now make us feel happy and satisfied.

surrender to what you cannot control

Camper or van or other kind of tiny living, like all things, is not properly represented on social media. If you find yourself scrolling through #vanlife and feel like those images are realistic, you are mistaken. Following nearly every beautiful moment, every bucolic view, every marvel of nature, and every cozy, peaceful night's sleep is an aggravation. The greatest lesson I've learned through this lifestyle is to just let it be. If I do my best and constantly tell myself it's not good enough, what is the point of trying? If I do my best and remind myself that's what I'm doing, then I begin to feel the flow. It's easier just to surrender.

I'll spend an hour cleaning the camper and it will be back to messy the following day, and that's all right. That's how things are. We'll wake up to rain and some will have leaked from the ceiling, and that's all right too. Mac's feet will get muddy and he will jump up on the bed, the raccoons will knock over the garbage cans yet again, and I'll find ants in the sugar bag. That's it and that's life, and if I allow those little things to weigh heavily on me, they turn into one giant burden that holds me down. This life isn't about perfection, and it's rarely tidy. It's about basking in beautiful imperfection, breathing in fresh air, and feeling the sun on your skin. When those things become the priority, the little inconveniences don't matter as much, and you can become present and grateful for what really matters.

EASY OUTDOOR COOKING

on fire

Even when I was little, I never liked that building a fire was considered a man's job. Maybe this wasn't the case for you, but for me, every time I was in a group of people enjoying a fire, whether inside or out, it was always a fire built by a man. Why do Boy Scouts learn survival skills while Girl Scouts are best known for selling cookies? Why was building a fire always a man's job?

When we moved into the woods, I really started working on my fire skills. Sean would challenge me to light a fire for dinner with one match, and over time, I could often do it. I collected the dry wood, I split the logs, I found the kindling, and I fed the fire until it grew and grew. I also took notes while watching our tree surgeon burning limbs. He did it fearlessly and with such finesse. You could tell he had been doing it for most of his life. I asked him questions and watched him closely. He showed me how to do it safely and how to let go of unnecessary fears. I practiced and practiced, burning brush while we cleared our house site and burning oak and maple to cook dinner over. I built fires over and over and over again.

my outdoor cooking setup

First things first—I'd like to make it clear that I am not rich. I do not have much money. When I first started writing this book, I thought, "Oh wow, I'm going to get all these wild grilling contraptions." Adjustable grates, tripods with chains for holding pots over the flame, a plancha in every size—I wanted them all. I'd like to think that someday I'll have all of those things on hand to play with, but the truth is, I couldn't afford them. It's worked out for the best, however, because I want this book to feel accessible, and how could I write a book of truly accessible camping recipes if I couldn't afford the tools? And so, once again, I've surrendered to what I cannot control and made a choice to lean into it.

Every single campfire recipe in this book can be cooked on a grate, in a cast-iron pan, or in a Dutch oven. That's it—because that's all I've got. And it's more than enough. The only recipe in this book that does not require one of those tools calls for an eighteen-dollar purchase from a hardware store. As with camper life in general, I've found a great deal of freedom in this simplification of things. Plus, I feel proud of being resourceful, of only using what we have, and of finding ways to make the best food I can without much limitation. Now that I've gotten that out of the way, here's what you'll need.

the grill

"Grilling" is a term used loosely. Generally, people think of it as cooking anything over intense heat, typically outside. In this book, to distinguish between cooking over a roaring campfire and smoldering charcoal, I use "grilling" to refer to cooking something over charcoal on a grill grate. I tend to use a grate over coals in my firepit or my charcoal grill; that to me is grilling. I did not use a gas grill for these recipes but of course I consider that grilling as well, and these recipes will work perfectly on your gas grill if that's what you're working with. I have nothing against gas grills and adore their convenience but prefer charcoal because of the smoky flavor it gives whatever you're cooking. Anything cooked on a charcoal grill, gas grill, or a grill grate over coals in a firepit is "grilling" to me.

essential tools

A grill. A charcoal grill, gas grill, or a grill grate over a firepit. Any of these will do.

Good charcoal. I like natural hardwood lump charcoal, such as Royal Oak. I don't believe in using briquets that are filled with chemicals, and I like relying on a brand that I can find pretty much anywhere.

Charcoal chimney. This makes the process so much easier. I love using a chimney because I can move on and prep other things while my charcoal is preparing itself.

Dry firewood. Make sure the firewood you're cooking with is dry and safe. You can't use just any wood you have lying around. It has to be natural. Never use construction scraps like pressure-treated wood, as they can be extremely toxic. I use oak and maple because that's what we have on our property.

An axe. Once you have your firewood, you'll need to break it down with an axe. Plenty of kindling is the key to a good campfire. Split your logs into thin pieces so you can get the fire going quickly.

Reliable lighters. Have a couple of lighters around. There's nothing worse than being stuck with a dead lighter.

Grill grate. I'm pretty sure the grate I use was found at the dump by Sean's dad. One man's trash is another man's first cookbook deal. I do prefer to use a grate with bars that aren't too far apart. I look for ¼-½-inch bars that are ¼-½ inch apart. That way little things like cherry tomatoes or snap peas won't slip through the cracks. It doesn't need to be anything flashy. Just make sure it's solid cast iron, and if you treat it well and clean it properly, it'll last a lifetime.

Cast-iron frying pan. This is the pan I use the most in my cooking (see page 21), and I couldn't have written this book without it. It is the most important tool a cook can take out into the woods.

Cast-iron Dutch oven. Being able to place it directly into the firepit and cover it with coals means whatever is inside cooks perfectly from all angles. It is ideal for roasting a whole chicken; simmering big, hearty soups and stews; and even baking.

Enameled cast-iron Dutch oven or braiser. I use the same Le Creuset Dutch oven that I've used in every kitchen I've ever had (see page 21). It's not too big for the camper stove top, and although it gets a little dirty sometimes, it also works wonderfully over the campfire.

Welding gloves. A frying pan placed directly over a large flame will get ripping hot very quickly. It's important you have proper hand protection when retrieving extremely hot pots and pans from the fire. So be sure to get a good-quality pair of welding gloves. I've purchased cheap ones in the past and learned the very hard way that they simply don't protect your hands from the intense heat. Even a good pair is reasonably priced, so just avoid the very cheapest.

Long, sturdy grilling tongs. A reliable set of classic grilling tongs is a must. I use them almost every time I grill, and I'm sure you do too.

camper
breakfast

There's something sacred about cooking breakfast when you live in a camper in the woods. Choosing this lifestyle means choosing slower living. Starting each day by meditatively making something good to eat is a reminder that you've chosen a way of life that allows you to let go of rushing out of the house and shoving a granola bar into your mouth because you are late to the office. Instead, step outside to a beautiful fall morning, cozy in a wool sweater and socks and with a coffee in hand, to make a fire. Feel the morning light on your face as you collect kindling and chop firewood. Watch the smoke slowly rise through the trees. Smell butter browning in a cast-iron pan. Have another cup of coffee because you don't have to be any particular place just yet. That's a nice feeling.

I'm not saying I no longer experience stressful mornings. I definitely do. But no matter how much nature may be fighting against us that day, I still relish no longer having to catch the subway for work. If you're camping for a short period of time, maybe just for a weekend, I'd suggest doing your best to wake up early each day. Listen to the birds, to the wind, to everything around you. Notice how the warmth of the sun is different in the morning. Notice your body, your breathing, your mind. Notice that you are a part of everything you feel and hear and see around you. I find that taking an early-morning minute to practice this kind of thing really helps me feel more comfortable in my mind and body. A moment like this, right before making a delicious campfire breakfast? It's a wonderful thing.

Bacon, Eggs, and Beans

This hearty breakfast came together when I was daydreaming about what I thought cowboys in the past ate out on the range: something warming and heavy and with beans as the star of the show. I learned that if you're craving baked beans but only have a can of plain pinto beans, you can easily transform them with some bacon fat and a little brown sugar.

Heat a large cast-iron frying pan over medium-high heat. Lay the bacon slices in the hot pan and fry, flipping once, until golden and crisp on both sides, 5–7 minutes. Transfer the bacon to a plate, leaving the fat in the pan.

Add the onion to the pan and cook, stirring often, until tender, about 5 minutes. Add the sugar and stir to mix with the onion. Add the beans, season with salt and pepper, and stir until well combined. Allow the bean mixture to cook, stirring occasionally, for 1–3 minutes to heat the beans and blend the flavors.

With a wooden spoon, create 5 small, evenly spaced, shallow hollows in the bean mixture and then carefully crack an egg into each hollow. Cook the eggs sunny side up by covering the pan with a lid or foil and removing it once the egg whites have set but the yolks are still runny, 2–3 minutes.

Break up the bacon slices, crumbling them on top of the eggs and beans, and then sprinkle everything with salt, pepper, and chives. Serve immediately directly from the pan, accompanied with toast.

Makes 4–5 servings

3–4 slices bacon

1 white onion, sliced

2 tablespoons light brown sugar

1 can (15 oz) pinto beans, drained and rinsed

Kosher salt and freshly cracked black pepper

5 eggs

Chopped fresh chives for garnish

Toasted bread for serving

Blueberry–Olive Oil Pancakes

I've never really liked pancakes. I've actually never even ordered them at a restaurant in my whole life. I'm a dessert person but not a sweets-for-a-meal person. Sean, however, is the biggest pancake fan around, and boy does he make great ones! He taught me a little secret that he gave me permission to share in this book: fry your pancakes in olive oil instead of butter. You'll add butter on top later, of course, but if you fry pancakes in olive oil, they get these incredible extra-crispy edges that I absolutely swoon for. These are not your big, spongy, fluffy IHOP pancakes. They are thin, delicate, and turn a deep golden brown. They're also absolutely bursting with blueberries because I just couldn't help myself.

In a large bowl, whisk together the flour, baking soda, and kosher salt with a fork. Add the buttermilk, eggs, and oil and whisk until combined. Mix in the blueberries and set the bowl near the stove.

Heat a large cast-iron frying pan over medium-high heat. When the pan is hot, add enough oil to lightly coat the bottom. When the oil is shimmering, add a ladleful (about ½ cup) of the batter to the pan. Cook until bubbles appear on the whole top surface of the pancake and the bottom is golden brown, about 3 minutes. Flip and cook until the second side is golden brown, 1–2 minutes longer. Transfer to a plate. Repeat until you have used all the batter, adding more oil to the pan as needed to prevent sticking.

Serve the pancakes with butter, maple syrup, and a sprinkle of flaky salt.

Makes about 8 pancakes

1 cup all-purpose flour

1 teaspoon baking soda

Big pinch of kosher salt

1½ cups buttermilk

2 eggs

2 tablespoons olive oil, plus lots more for cooking

½–1 cup blueberries

Butter, pure maple syrup, and flaky salt for serving

Spiced Honey-Roasted Peanut Granola

Granola feels like the official snack of camper living. This one is sweet, salty, heavily spiced, and an appetizing deep golden brown. It's perfect enjoyed with yogurt, milk, or straight up by the fistful while hiking.

Preheat the oven to 350°F. Line a sheet pan with parchment paper.

Pile the peanuts and oats on the parchment-lined pan, top with the honey and apple pie spice, and mix with your hands until all the ingredients are evenly distributed. Spread the mixture in a thin layer, then drizzle evenly with a little oil and sprinkle with the salt.

Bake the granola until golden brown and fragrant, about 20 minutes. Let the granola cool completely on the pan (about 20 minutes), then break into pieces and serve.

Note: *Apple pie spice, a mixture of ground cinnamon, allspice, and nutmeg, can be purchased in well-stocked markets. Or you can make your own, using 2 parts cinnamon, 2 parts allspice, and 1 part nutmeg.*

Makes about 6 servings

1 cup honey-roasted peanuts

1 cup old-fashioned rolled oats

2 tablespoons honey

1 tablespoon apple pie spice (see Note)

Olive oil for drizzling

Big pinch of kosher salt

Tongore Home Fries

The Tongore Trading Post was a small convenience store in a gas station near my childhood home. It was actually the only store in Olivebridge. Along with a few aisles of snacks and basic kitchen staples, it had a little sun-filled dining room decorated with Native American artwork collecting dust. Sometimes as a treat, our family would go there for breakfast, where a very straightforward menu of eggs, pancakes, sausages, and the like was offered. I obsessively ordered the home fries. They were salty, greasy, and the perfect mix of potatoes, peppers, and onions. This recipe is a re-creation of that childhood favorite because an ideal camp breakfast always includes potatoes alongside your eggs.

Heat a large cast-iron frying pan over medium-high heat and add 2 tablespoons of the butter. When the butter melts and starts to bubble, add the onion and cook, stirring often, until soft, about 5 minutes. Add the bell peppers and cook, stirring often, until soft and the onions are golden, about 5 minutes. Add the potatoes and stir to mix everything together well. Allow the vegetables to cook undisturbed until they begin to form a golden crust on the bottom, about 7 minutes.

Add the paprika and onion powder, season with salt and pepper, and cook, stirring occasionally, until the potatoes are crispy and golden brown, about 6 minutes. Add the remaining 2 tablespoons butter and toss everything together until the butter melts. Serve immediately.

Makes about 6 servings

4 tablespoons (½ stick) butter

1 large white onion, diced

1 green bell pepper, seeded and chopped

1 red bell pepper, seeded and chopped

6 Yukon gold potatoes, about 1½ lb, preboiled and cut into 1-inch cubes

1 tablespoon smoked paprika

1 tablespoon onion powder

Kosher salt and freshly cracked black pepper

Wild Mushroom, Egg, and Cheese Sandwiches

I used to be terrified of foraging mushrooms, and I still kinda am. But I have a select few that I now feel comfortable picking for consumption because they really can't be mistaken for anything else: morels, chanterelles, and, the most common in my area, gorgeous oyster mushrooms.

If you're not comfortable foraging, *don't do it*. Never do something with such risk that you aren't 100 percent sure of! Fortunately, most farm stands and markets in the Hudson Valley carry a wide variety of wild mushrooms. With luck, sources in your area will do the same.

This recipe can be prepared outdoors or in. If cooking outdoors, light a campfire and place the grate over a section of the firepit with medium-high heat. Heat a large cast-iron frying pan over medium-high heat on the stove top or grate. Add a pat of butter and allow to melt. When the butter starts to bubble, add the thyme and mushrooms and allow them to cook, stirring occasionally, until the mushrooms are golden brown and crispy, 10–15 minutes. Transfer the mushrooms to a bowl, sprinkle with salt and pepper, and set aside. Discard the thyme.

If you're cooking outside, toast the bread over the fire on the grate, flip, top each slice with a slice of cheese, and heat until it is melty. If you're cooking indoors, preheat the broiler. Line up the bread slices on a sheet pan, slide the pan under the broiler, and toast, flipping once, until golden brown on both sides. Once the second side is toasted, top each piece with a slice of cheese and leave just until it melts.

While the bread is toasting, return the pan to medium-high heat and add a bit more butter. When the butter melts and starts to bubble, crack in the eggs. Cook the eggs sunny side up until the whites are just set and the yolks are still runny, about 4 minutes. Season with salt and pepper and remove from the heat.

To assemble the sandwiches, place each egg on a cheesy piece of toast, top each egg with half of the mushrooms, and then close each sandwich with a second slice of toast, cheesy side down. Cut in half and eat immediately, accompanied with hot sauce.

Makes 2 sandwiches

Butter for cooking

Few fresh thyme sprigs

About 2 cups wild mushrooms (I like oyster, king trumpet, and chanterelle), brushed clean and halved lengthwise if large

Kosher salt and freshly cracked black pepper

4 slices multigrain bread

4 slices Swiss cheese (Cheddar is excellent too)

2 eggs

Hot sauce for serving

Raspberry Buttermilk Breakfast Cake

It's just a big pancake—a big pancake that's perfect for your campfire. There's a time and place for flipping li'l silver dollar pancakes, and I love doing it, but I'm putting this recipe here as a reminder that there is an easier way. This giant pancake is fun for a crowd, and you don't have to worry about anything getting cold like you do when you're cooking a batch of regular pancakes. Just slather with butter, drench with syrup, and slice like a cake.

In a large bowl, whisk together the flour, baking soda, and salt with a fork. Add the buttermilk and eggs and whisk until just combined. In a small bowl, mash the raspberries with the fork and set aside (this is optional, but I feel that adding the berries whole makes the pancake look like a pepperoni pizza).

Heat a large cast-iron frying pan over medium-high heat. Add a pat of butter, allow to melt, and then swirl the pan to coat the bottom evenly with the butter to prevent the pancake from sticking. Pour in all of the pancake batter and cover the pan with its lid. Allow to cook for about 5 minutes, then remove the lid, scatter the raspberries evenly on top, and re-cover. Continue to cook until the pancake is cooked all the way through (test by inserting a fork into the pancake, and if it comes out dry, it's ready), about 10 minutes longer.

Uncover and top with butter and maple syrup. Serve directly from the pan, cut into wedges.

Makes about 4 servings

1½ cups all-purpose flour

1 teaspoon baking soda

Big pinch of kosher salt

1½ cups buttermilk

2 eggs

1½ cups raspberries

Butter for cooking and serving

Pure maple syrup for serving

Summer Tomato Sandwiches

Like many, I dream of a tomato sandwich all year long. It's a meal that signifies a season that's all about pleasure: every swimming hole is at its warmest, swarms of flashing fireflies fill the night sky, and the perfect start to the day is juices from an heirloom-tomato sandwich running down your arms as you happily struggle to contain the glorious mess of it all. My family ate lots of tomato sandwiches in the summer. We would load up dark pieces of toast with massive slices of scarlet tomato, creamy mayo, and an absolute staple: Herbamare, a seemingly forgotten "herbed sea salt" that is the taste and smell of my childhood. It's hard to describe the flavor, but it's definitely celery salt–forward and highly addictive. It's still available, mostly in little mom-and-pop health food stores, and I dress every summer tomato I eat with it.

To me, this sandwich is breakfast food. It's quick and simple and involves toast, but it also makes a great snack, lunch, or dinner, and during peak tomato season, I'm more than happy to eat this for all of the above.

Toast your bread. If you've got your campfire going, grill it on the grate over the fire—a real treat. If you don't have a fire, toast it under the broiler.

While the bread is toasting, make the spread. In a small bowl, mix together the mayonnaise, chives, lemon zest, and lemon juice and season to taste with pepper and Herbamare.

Once the toast is ready, slather one side of each slice with the spread. Stack as many tomato slices as you like on half of the bread slices, then close with a second bread slice, spread side down. Cut in half and eat immediately. Remember, it's not a real summer tomato sandwich without plenty of dripping juice.

Makes 4 sandwiches

FOR THE SANDWICHES

8 slices sourdough bread

2 large beefsteak or other large heirloom tomatoes, sliced

FOR THE SPREAD

½ cup mayonnaise

1 tablespoon chopped fresh chives

Grated zest of 1 lemon

Juice of ½ lemon

Freshly cracked black pepper

Herbamare for seasoning

Veg-Heavy Frittata

I love a frittata to feed a crowd, and this one is perfect for a family camping trip. My favorite frittatas are bursting with vegetables. The spring produce I use in this recipe is wonderful but feel free to improvise per season—zucchini, peppers, and cherry tomatoes in the summer, or hearty greens like kale and collards in the fall and winter. Even roasted squash would be a fantastic addition in the colder months.

Prepare a charcoal or gas grill for direct cooking over medium-high heat.

In a large bowl, whisk together the eggs and set aside. Coat a large cast-iron frying pan with oil and set it on the grill. When the pan is hot, add the potatoes, cut side down, and cook undisturbed, until golden and crispy, about 5 minutes. Mix in the leek, asparagus, and mushrooms, season with salt and pepper, and cook, stirring often, until all the vegetables are tender, 5–10 minutes.

Add the whole basil leaves, whole parsley leaves, and butter, then stir. As soon as the herbs are slightly wilted and the butter has melted, make sure the vegetable mixture is spread evenly in the pan. Pour in the eggs and swirl the pan to ensure they are evenly distributed. Season with salt and pepper and sprinkle the Cheddar evenly over the top. Cover the grill and cook until the eggs have set and the cheese has melted, about 3 minutes.

Remove from the grill and top with chopped basil and parsley. Serve directly from the pan, cut into wedges and accompanied with hot sauce.

Makes about 6 servings

8 eggs

Olive oil for cooking

2 cups little potatoes, preboiled and halved

1 leek, white and tender green tops, chopped

1 cup trimmed and chopped asparagus

2 cups sliced mushrooms

Kosher salt and freshly cracked black pepper

½ cup fresh basil leaves, plus more, finely chopped, for finishing

½ cup fresh flat-leaf parsley leaves, plus more, finely chopped, for finishing

3 tablespoons butter

2 cups shredded sharp Cheddar cheese

Hot sauce for serving

Big Green Smoothie

Right after college, I got a job at Peacefood, a wonderful little vegan café on Manhattan's Upper West Side. I mostly worked the counter, boxing baked goods and to-go orders, and eventually I was trained as a juicer, which was really exciting, as the juices and smoothies were like nothing I'd ever had before. One in particular always stood out to me because of its high nutritional value and surprisingly lovely flavor. The smoothie was called the "green power." It was so many years ago—and it's still my favorite smoothie. This is my riff on that extremely memorable drink. Look for good-quality orange juice. I use Natalie's, which is based in Florida and is shipped around the country.

Combine all the ingredients in a large glass or metal cup and blend with an immersion blender until smooth. Pour into glasses and serve.

Note: *If you don't have a freezer, use room-temperature fruit and add 1 cup ice.*

Makes 2 servings

1 banana, frozen (see Note), peeled, and cut up

½ cup frozen berries, any kind (see Note)

Large handful of dark, leafy greens, such as spinach or kale

1 cup high-quality orange juice

1 tablespoon spirulina

1–2 teaspoons pure maple syrup

Banana and Coffee Smoothie

A few years ago, Sean and I spent a couple of weeks surfing in Nosara, Costa Rica. Every morning before a day at the beach, we'd visit a small smoothie stand near Playa Guiones for a perfect drink that combined our morning coffee with breakfast. This smoothie is a re-creation of that daily ritual. The milk and banana will hold you over until your next meal, and there's enough coffee in there to wake you up. A really nice "two birds with one stone" breakfast.

Combine all the ingredients in a large glass or metal cup and blend with an immersion blender until smooth. Pour into 1 or 2 glasses and serve.

Note: *If you don't have a freezer, use a room-temperature banana and add 1 cup ice.*

Makes 1–2 servings

1 cup cold brewed coffee

½ cup soy milk or oat milk

1 banana, frozen (see Note), peeled, and cut up

1 tablespoon pure maple syrup

1 teaspoon unsweetened cocoa powder

Pinch of kosher salt

Cooler Gravlax

Yes, in a cooler, in the woods, with a thermometer and some ice you can cure your own fish. I love gravlax, and curing my own made me feel like such a champion. You can get crazy with your spice-and-herb variations, but this is my go-to recipe that I encourage you to try, camping or not. Serve the gravlax with bagels, cream cheese, red onion slices, capers, and lemon wedges; on toast with goat cheese and avocado, with eggs, with rice, in a salad. The list goes on.

Makes about 10 servings

½ cup kosher salt

½ cup sugar

½ cup dill fronds, chopped

Grated zest of 1 lemon

1 tablespoon freshly cracked black pepper

2 lb skin-on salmon or steelhead trout fillet, in a single piece

In a small bowl, whisk together the salt, sugar, dill, lemon zest, and pepper with a fork, then set aside. Pat the fish down with a paper towel, making sure it looks clean and is rid of any bones. Roll plastic wrap out on a sheet pan and lay the fish, skin side down, on top. Cover the entire surface of the fish evenly with the salt mixture, then wrap the salmon tightly in the plastic wrap. Poke a few holes in the plastic wrap to drain any liquid the fish may release as it cures. Place the fish, still on the sheet pan, in the fridge or on ice in the cooler. Place a thermometer in the cooler so you can track the temperature, making sure it doesn't exceed 40°F.

Leave the salmon undisturbed for about 12 hours, then check to see if the sheet pan is holding any liquid. If it is, drain off the liquid and return the fish, still on the sheet pan, to the cooler. Allow the fish to cure for at least 24 hours (you can leave it for 48 or even 72 hours if you like).

When you're ready to eat the gravlax, remove the plastic wrap, thoroughly rinse the salt mixture off the fish, and pat the fish dry with a paper towel. Place the salmon, skin side down, on a work surface. Starting at the tail end of the fillet and using a sharp chef's knife with the blade slightly angled toward the skin, carefully cut the skin away from the flesh. Then, holding the chef's knife at a roughly 45-degree angle and starting near the tail end, cut toward the tail end, slicing the fillet as thinly as possible to serve.

everything-on-the-grill meals

My biggest camper cooking mistakes have happened when I've tried to spread out my cooking. To have the oven going, the stove top on, and a fire outside all for one meal feels like way too much. I like to keep everything as close together as I can, and sometimes cooking on the grill and incorporating the cast-iron frying pan or making a sauce with a grilled component that goes on a piece of grilled protein makes me feel clever. With a large enough grill grate, you have the ability to use different cooking methods over the very same flame, and that feels as efficient as it is fun.

Campfire Bucatini with Charred Tomato Sauce

Never did I ever expect myself to absolutely fall in love with a pasta dish on the fire. Pasta seemed like a meal to be kept in the camper, but wow, that's simply not true. The flavor that charring the tomatoes adds is unreal. It's smoky in a way that tastes like bacon or pancetta. And the reheated leftovers somehow taste even smokier. This recipe calls for cooking the pasta straight in the sauce instead of boiling it in water. I know that can seem blasphemous, and not all pasta shapes will work for this recipe. For example, in my experience, orecchiette should always be boiled first because the little shapes tend to stack together, making it difficult to cook them evenly directly in sauce. However, bucatini is made for this method. The thick spaghetti-like pasta does an incredible job of sucking up all the flavors while cooking evenly and perfectly al dente. If you think pasta doesn't have a place on the campfire, I urge you to make this recipe the next time you're cooking outside.

Light your campfire and top with a grate.

Place the cherry tomatoes directly on the grate of your campfire, arranging them on just half of the grate. Allow them to char on one side and then turn them carefully with tongs to char on the second side. Place a Dutch oven next to the tomatoes as they char and let it reach medium-high heat. When the pot is hot, coat the bottom with oil. When the oil is shimmering, add the anchovies, garlic, and tomato paste. When the garlic just starts to brown on the edges, stir everything together with a wooden spoon and then add all the cherry tomatoes to the pot and stir again, bursting some tomatoes here and there. Allow the mixture to cook (it should be bubbling) until it shows signs of reduction, which should take about 5 minutes. Season with salt and pepper.

Once the sauce has thickened, add the water, Parmesan cube, basil, and bucatini, cover the pot with its lid, and allow the pasta to cook in the sauce for about 10 minutes, stirring once or twice to prevent the sauce from sticking to the bottom of the pot.

Remove the lid, add the butter, and stir constantly until the pasta is al dente. This should take no more than 5–7 minutes. Garnish with the grated Parmesan, chopped basil, and a grind or two of pepper and serve immediately, directly from the pot.

Makes 4–6 servings

2 pints cherry tomatoes (about 1½ lb)

Olive oil for cooking

2 anchovy fillets in olive oil

2 cloves garlic, sliced

1 tablespoon tomato paste

Kosher salt and freshly cracked black pepper

2 cups water

2-inch cube Parmesan cheese, plus grated Parmesan for garnish

3 fresh basil sprigs, plus chopped leaves for garnish

1 package (1 lb) bucatini

2 tablespoons butter

Seared Mushrooms with Cacio e Pepe Polenta

Earthy mushrooms served over creamy and comforting polenta is an ideal stick-to-your-ribs meal for the winter months. You can, of course, prepare this meal on the stove top, but the mushrooms take on a fantastic smoky flavor when cooked over a campfire or on a grill. If you are lucky enough to have leftovers, they're great served with a fried egg on top in the morning.

Prepare a charcoal or gas grill for direct cooking over medium-high heat. Or light a campfire and place a grate over a section of the firepit with medium-high heat.

To make the mushrooms, set a large cast-iron frying pan on the grill or campfire grate. When the pan is hot, coat the bottom of the pan with oil. When the oil is shimmering, add the shallots and cook, stirring, until tender, 5–10 minutes. Add the mushrooms, stir until coated with oil, and then cook, stirring occasionally, until golden brown, 10–15 minutes.

Once the mushrooms are cooked, pour in the wine and deglaze the pan, stirring to dislodge any browned bits from the pan bottom. Add the rosemary and butter, season with salt and pepper, and cook everything together, stirring frequently, for about 5 minutes, to melt the butter and blend the flavors. Cover the pan with a lid and set aside on a cooler part of the grill or campfire grate.

To make the polenta, set a Dutch oven over the hottest part of the grill or campfire grate, add the water, and bring to a boil. Move the Dutch oven to a cooler area and slowly stream in the polenta while stirring constantly. Then continue to cook, stirring frequently, for 5 minutes. The polenta will thicken, and bubbles will slowly form and burst. Remove from the heat, cover, and let stand for 1–2 minutes. Uncover, add the Parmesan, butter, and pepper, season with salt, and stir until the cheese and butter melt.

To serve, scatter the mushroom mixture over the polenta and top with more Parmesan and a dusting of parsley and lemon zest. Serve immediately, directly from the pot.

Makes 6–8 servings

FOR THE MUSHROOMS

Olive oil for cooking

2 shallots, thinly sliced

8 cups mixed fresh mushrooms (about 1 lb), brushed clean and roughly chopped

½ cup dry white wine

3 fresh rosemary sprigs

4 tablespoons (½ stick) butter

Kosher salt and freshly cracked black pepper

FOR THE POLENTA

6 cups water

2 cups instant polenta

1 cup grated Parmesan cheese, plus more for garnish

6 tablespoons butter

1 teaspoon freshly cracked black pepper

Kosher salt

Chopped fresh flat-leaf parsley and grated lemon zest for garnish

Pearl Couscous with Mixed Vegetables and Feta

I could eat pasta or grains layered with vegetables and bright and briny feta and olives every day. Use this recipe as an easy side for nearly any protein, mix it with leafy greens to make it a full-blown salad, eat it warm when the vegetables come right off the heat, or chill it in your cooler or fridge and bring it on a hike the next day for a perfect little mountaintop lunch.

Prepare your charcoal or gas grill for direct cooking over medium-high heat.

Put the garlic cloves in the center of a square of aluminum foil, coat them with oil, and crumple the foil into a sealed ball. Place the foil packet on the grill grate. Next, coat the eggplant(s), carrots, onion, and zucchini with oil and season with salt and pepper. Set the vegetables on the grill grate and grill, using tongs to rotate them frequently, until they are tender all the way through and a bit charred on all sides, about 20 minutes. Rotate the garlic packet occasionally as you tend the vegetables.

Transfer the vegetables and garlic packet to a cutting board. When the vegetables are cool enough to handle, trim them as needed. Remove the garlic from the foil and squeeze each clove out of its skin. Add the garlic to the vegetables and coarsely chop everything together.

Spoon the couscous onto a platter and cover it with the vegetables. Top evenly with the feta, oregano, and lemon zest and juice. Drizzle with oil, season with salt and pepper, and serve.

Makes 4–6 servings

5 cloves garlic, unpeeled

Olive oil for coating and drizzling

3 small or 1 large eggplant

5 small or 2 large carrots, peeled

1 red onion, peeled and cut in half

1 zucchini

Kosher salt and freshly cracked black pepper

6 cups cooked pearl couscous, cooked according to package directions and kept warm

1 cup crumbled feta cheese

2 tablespoons fresh oregano leaves

Grated zest and juice of 1 lemon

Grilled Bread with Goat Cheese and Charred Peppers

This is a routine breakfast, lunch, or snack for me. Elegant but not at all fussy, it's also a wonderful little appetizer. I typically cook off a large number of peppers, dress them in the marinade, and stick them into a container in the cooler so I can have this perfect little meal anytime.

I find anchovies are the best partner here, but you can substitute sardines, smoked trout, some smoked salmon, or a fried egg.

Prepare a charcoal or gas grill for direct cooking over medium-high heat. Or light a campfire and place a grate over a section of the firepit with medium-high heat.

Halve and seed the peppers, then cut the halves into pieces easy to maneuver over the fire and large enough not to fall through the bars of the grate. Place the peppers on the grill or campfire grate and cook, turning occasionally, until they are soft and a little charred from the flame. This should take 10–20 minutes, depending on how large your fire is. When they are ready, transfer them to a large bowl.

Add the oil, lemon zest and juice, vinegar, garlic, and oregano to the peppers, season with salt and pepper, and then turn the peppers in the mixture to coat evenly. Set aside to marinate while you toast the bread.

Grill the sourdough over the fire, turning once, until it develops grill marks on both sides. Remove the bread from the fire and immediately spread one-fourth of the goat cheese evenly on one side of each slice.

Arrange the cheese-topped toasts on a large plate and top each one with one-fourth of the marinated peppers, adding some of the marinade along with the peppers. Top each toast with an anchovy fillet and serve immediately.

Makes 2–4 servings

4 peppers (see headnote)

¼ cup olive oil

Grated zest and juice of 1 lemon

Splash of vinegar (red wine, champagne, or apple cider will work great)

2 cloves garlic, grated

1 tablespoon fresh oregano leaves

Kosher salt and freshly cracked black pepper

4 slices sourdough bread

¼ lb fresh goat cheese

4 anchovy fillets in olive oil

Fancy Hot Dogs with Fried Leeks and Sauerkraut

If you were expecting hot dogs with caviar or foie gras, I'm sorry to disappoint, but these are outrageously good. Taking the time to cook a delicious topping for your hot dog makes it special. And to me, fried leeks and sauerkraut are the most special of them all. Although eating hot dogs with just mustard and relish is always fun, crowning them with something substantial turns them into a satisfying meal.

Prepare a charcoal or gas grill for direct cooking over medium-high heat.

Set a large cast-iron frying pan on the grill. When the pan is hot, coat the bottom with oil. When the oil is shimmering, add the leek and cook, stirring occasionally, until golden and crispy, about 10 minutes.

While the leek is cooking, arrange the hot dogs on the grill grate and cook, turning as needed, until crisp and charred with grill marks on each side, then remove from the grill.

When the leek is ready, transfer it to a bowl. Then add the sauerkraut to the pan and cook, stirring often, until any liquid is gone and it begins to brown, about 10 minutes. Once the sauerkraut has browned, return the leek to the pan, add the butter, season with salt and pepper, and stir until the butter melts.

Finally, set the hot dog buns, split side down, on the grate and grill until toasty, then remove from the grill.

Assemble the hot dogs and buns as usual and top each with a generous heap of the sauerkraut leek mixture. Add mustard and ketchup too if you like. Serve immediately.

Makes 6 hot dogs

Olive oil for cooking

1 large leek, sliced

6 hot dogs

2 cups drained sauerkraut

2 tablespoons butter

Kosher salt and freshly cracked black pepper

6 hot dog buns, preferably potato buns

Mustard and ketchup for serving (optional)

Mussels in Red Sauce with Fried Garlic Bread

A big pot of mussels cooked over the fire is such a treat. But the idea of mussels without a large hunk of crusty bread for soaking up the sauce makes me sad. I love the idea of dumping them over bread so it soaks up every bit it can. One of my favorite restaurants in the entire world, Hart's in Brooklyn, does this famously with clams. Their clam toast is one of those plates of food I always have in the back of my mind—the kind that every time you're about to cook something makes you ask yourself, "Can anything I make ever be as good as that?" And now, under that influence, nine times out of ten when I'm eating shellfish, I dump it over fried bread. Luckily for me, it's a fantastically cozy thing to prepare on the grill or over the campfire. I bet you'll agree.

Prepare your charcoal or gas grill for direct cooking over medium heat. Or light a campfire and place a grate over a section of the firepit with medium heat.

Set a Dutch oven on the grill or campfire grate. When the pot is hot, coat the bottom with oil. When the oil is shimmering, add 2 bread slices (or as many as will fit in a single layer) and fry, flipping once, until golden brown on both sides. It should take no more than a couple of minutes on each side. Remove from the pot and rub each slice on both sides with a garlic clove. Repeat with the remaining bread, adding more oil if needed, then set the bread aside.

Add the tomatoes to the pan and cook, stirring occasionally, until they soften and burst, 5–10 minutes. When the juices from the tomatoes are bubbling and beginning to thicken, add the tomato paste and stir. Let the tomato mixture cook, stirring occasionally, for 1–2 minutes, then add the capers and cook, stirring occasionally, for another 1–2 minutes. Pour in the wine and deglaze the pot, stirring to dislodge any browned bits from the pot bottom, then simmer until slightly reduced, about 5 minutes. Season with salt and pepper.

Add the mussels, discarding any that are cracked or fail to close to the touch. Cover the pot with its lid (or a sheet pan if you don't have a lid) and cook for 1–2 minutes. Uncover, stir gently to move any unopened mussels to the bottom, re-cover, and continue to cook until all the mussels are open, 2–3 minutes longer. Discard any mussels that failed to open.

Arrange the garlic bread on a large platter and pour the mussels and their sauce over the top. Finish with the lemon zest and juice, a drizzle of oil, and a dusting of parsley. Serve right away.

Makes about 4 servings

Olive oil for cooking and finishing

4 slices good bread (such as sourdough or peasant)

2 cloves garlic

1 pint cherry tomatoes (about ¾ lb)

1 tablespoon tomato paste

2 tablespoons capers, drained

1 cup dry white wine

Kosher salt and freshly cracked black pepper

2 lb mussels, rinsed, scrubbed, and errant beards removed

Grated zest and juice of 1 lemon

Chopped fresh flat-leaf parsley for garnish

Clams with Lemongrass and Coconut Milk

Leftover rice is a wonderful thing to have on hand. Whenever Sean and I would pack up the camper and go to stay with Marko, Sean's dad, I'd use his rice cooker to make a giant batch of rice. I'm not a fan of appliances that really do only one thing, but hot damn, a rice cooker is the ultimate exception. I would probably have a little one in the camper if it weren't for Marko already having one I can use. And what's the very best thing to do with it? For me, any blanket of saucy and creamy and stewy is ideal. If I have white rice in the cooler, I am 100 percent making this comforting meal. It's lightning fast to put together (if you're going camping, make the rice at home and bring it along, or just make it on your camper stove top like a true purist), and it's an absolute joy to cook over a fire. Be sure to dispose of your shells properly and far away from your campsite. I've heard that woodland creatures love this recipe too. If you don't have rice, this dish is just as delicious served over toasted sourdough or peasant bread.

Prepare a charcoal or gas grill for direct cooking over medium-high heat. Or light a campfire and place a grate over a section of the firepit with medium-high heat.

Set a Dutch oven on the grill or campfire grate. When the pot is hot, add the coconut oil. When the oil has melted, add the lemongrass. It will crackle and hiss a bit, which is OK. Allow the lemongrass to infuse the oil, turning the pieces occasionally, until crispy and brown, 5–10 minutes. Once the lemongrass is deeply browned, remove and discard it.

Add the garlic and ginger and cook, stirring, until fragrant, about 1 minute. Add the coconut milk, season with salt and pepper, and stir together. Add the clams, stir together again, then cover the pot and cook until the clams have opened and the pot is steaming, 5–10 minutes. Discard any clams that failed to open.

Stir together one more time, the add the cilantro and squeeze in the lime. Serve immediately, spooned over rice.

Note: *To reheat cooked rice, bring a cast-iron pan to medium heat on the grill or over a campfire. Coat the pan with a neutral oil, then add the rice along with a splash of water. Cook, stirring frequently, until the rice is fully warmed and steaming, about 5 minutes.*

Makes 2 servings

3 tablespoons coconut oil

3 lemongrass stalks, root end and grassy tops trimmed off, then tough outer layers pulled off

3 cloves garlic, grated

1-inch piece fresh ginger, peeled and grated

1 can (13.5 oz) full-fat coconut milk

Kosher salt and freshly cracked black pepper

12 clams, such as cherrystone or littleneck, rinsed and scrubbed

Small handful of fresh cilantro sprigs, chopped

1 lime, halved

Hot cooked white rice for serving (see Note)

Grilled White Anchovy and Cured Black Olive Pizza

When I lived in Bushwick, I was only a few blocks from Ops and Roberta's. I'm a sucker for a Neopolitan-style pizza with creative toppings and this recipe satisfies that craving. You can of course make this pizza with store-bought sauce and shredded mozzarella, but the white anchovies, olives, and burrata make this pie feel like a night out in Bushwick.

To make the dough, combine the flour, yeast, and salt and stir to mix. While continuing to stir, slowly pour in the water, mixing until the mixture is evenly moistened. Add 2 tablespoons of the oil and continue to mix until a rough dough forms.

Turn the dough out onto a lightly floured work surface and knead until smooth, about 2 minutes. Wash and dry the bowl and coat the inside with the remaining 2 tablespoons oil. Form the dough into a ball, place in the bowl, cover with a kitchen towel, and let proof in a warm, draft-free spot until doubled in size, about 1 hour.

While you're waiting for the dough to proof, light your campfire, building your fire over the entire firepit and placing the grate over one section of the firepit.

To make the sauce, when the grate is hot, place all the tomatoes on it and allow them to char, rotating them with tongs so they color nicely on all sides. Once the tomatoes are jammy and very soft on the inside, transfer them to a bowl. Add the basil and a drizzle of oil, season with salt and pepper, and stir until mixed. Set aside.

When the dough is ready, cut it in half. Place one half in an airtight container and put it into the fridge or cooler to use another time. It will keep for 3–5 days.

Place a cast-iron frying pan directly on the hot coals in the firepit. While the pan heats, lightly dust the work surface and top with the remaining dough half. Using your hands, stretch the dough into a 12-inch round.

When the pan is very hot, place the dough round into the pan and cook the dough until the bottom begins to brown, 1–3 minutes. Flip the dough with a spatula and cover it with generous spoonfuls of the tomato sauce. Tear the burrata into pieces and scatter them over the sauce. Top with the anchovies, spacing them evenly, and then sprinkle with the olives. Cover the pan with its lid and allow to bake undisturbed until the cheese is melted and the bottom of the pizza is a deep golden brown, 3–5 minutes.

Uncover the pan and carefully transfer the pizza to a cutting board. Allow the pizza to cool for 2–3 minutes then top with the Parmesan. Cut into slices and serve.

Makes 2 servings

FOR THE DOUGH

3 cups all-purpose flour, plus more for the work surface

1 envelope (2¼ teaspoons) instant dry yeast

1 teaspoon kosher salt

1½ cups water

4 tablespoons olive oil

FOR THE SAUCE

1 pint cherry tomatoes (about ¾ lb)

¼ cup fresh basil leaves, chopped

Olive oil for drizzling

Kosher salt and freshly cracked black pepper

FOR TOPPING

1 package (8 oz) burrata cheese

5 white anchovy fillets

2 tablespoons chopped cured black olives

Grated Parmesan cheese for finishing

Striped Bass with Little Potatoes and Salsa Verde

Sean's dad, Marko, is a very good fisherman, and he is absolutely obsessive about striper season. Each spring, when the dogwoods are blooming, striped bass swim up the Hudson River to spawn. It's a very special time for Hudson Valley fishermen because they are saltwater fish swimming to our area in a body of water that you normally can't eat from. And the striped bass are *huge*, so it makes for a very exciting day on the boat. If you go fishing with Marko, you need to wake up at 4:00 a.m. He considers anything past 5:00 a.m. "sleeping in." We drive in the dark to the marina from which we launch his boat and set out to his special spot near the Kingston-Rhinecliff Bridge, arriving just as the sun comes up. There is nothing quite like being out on the water watching a sunrise. You feel overwhelmed by natural beauty as the world wakes up around you. I've been out striper fishing with Marko multiple times, but year after year I would get skunked—until finally this year, I caught my first striper. Here's how we prepared it.

Prepare a charcoal or gas grill for direct cooking over medium-high heat. Or light a campfire and place a grate over a section of the firepit with medium-high heat.

To make the salsa verde, set the tomatillos, onion, and jalapeño and poblano chiles on the grill or campfire grate. Grill the vegetables, using tongs to rotate them frequently, until they are charred on all sides and tender when pierced with a knife, 10–15 minutes. Transfer the vegetables to a bowl, cover the bowl, and let the vegetables steam, soften, and cool for about 5 minutes.

Once the vegetables have cooled down, chop them into very small pieces and return them to the bowl. Add the dill, cilantro, basil, lime zest and juice, and oil and stir to mix. Season with salt and pepper and set aside.

To cook the potatoes and fish, set a large cast-iron frying pan on the grill or campfire grate. When the pan is hot, coat the bottom with oil and add the potatoes. Allow the potatoes to cook, turning them occasionally, until they are hot all the way through, 3–5 minutes. Season with salt and pepper and transfer to a platter. Keep warm.

continues on next page

Makes 4 servings

FOR THE SALSA VERDE

4 tomatillos, papery husks removed and rinsed

1 white onion, peeled

2 jalapeño or serrano chiles, halved and seeded

1 poblano chile

1 tablespoon chopped fresh dill

1 tablespoon chopped fresh cilantro

1 tablespoon chopped fresh basil

Grated zest and juice of 2 limes

2–4 tablespoons olive oil

Kosher salt and freshly cracked black pepper

FOR THE POTATOES AND FISH

Olive oil for cooking

2 lb little potatoes, preboiled

Kosher salt and freshly cracked black pepper

2 lb skin-on striped bass or sea bass fillet

continued from previous page

If the pan is dry, add more oil to coat the bottom. When the oil is shimmering, add the fish, skin side down, and season the flesh side with salt and pepper. Cook until the skin is golden and very crispy and the flesh is beginning to turn opaque, about 7 minutes. Using tongs, flip the fish, season the skin side with salt and pepper, and continue to cook until the flesh is opaque, about 3 minutes longer. The timing depends on the thickness of the fillet; plan on about 10 minutes for a 1-inch-thick fillet.

Place the fish on top of the potatoes. Spoon the salsa verde on top and serve immediately.

Flank Steak and Brussels Sprout Salad Sandwiches

I love flank steak. It's inexpensive, easy to find, and when it's cooked and sliced right, I think it's one of the most delicious meats you can put into a sandwich. This one gets slathered with a beautiful Brussels sprout salad made with a sort of lazy Caesar-style dressing. I like thinly sliced raw Brussels sprouts, but some raw lacinato kale or savoy cabbage also works well here.

Put the flank steak in a shallow dish and pour the soy sauce evenly over it. Flip the steak to coat both sides evenly. Let the steak marinate as it comes to room temperature.

While the steak is marinating, prepare a charcoal or gas grill for direct cooking over medium-high heat.

To make the dressing, in a small bowl, whisk together the lemon juice, garlic, mayonnaise, and mustard with a fork. Then slowly stream in the oil while whisking constantly. Add the Parmesan to taste, season with salt and pepper, stir well, and set aside.

When the grill is ready, place the steak over the fire and grill until a golden crust forms on the first side, about 5 minutes. Flip the steak and continue to grill until a golden crust forms on the second side and an instant-read thermometer inserted into the center registers 130°–135°F for medium-rare, 3–4 minutes longer. At the same time, grill the bread slices, flipping them once, so they have lovely grill marks on both sides. If using rolls, grill the cut sides until etched with grill marks. As soon as the bread or rolls are ready, set them aside off the grill.

Transfer the steak to a cutting board and let rest for at least 5 minutes. While the steak is resting, put the Brussels sprouts into a medium bowl, pour the dressing over, and toss to coat evenly. Once the steak has rested, cut into very, very thin slices against the grain.

To assemble the sandwiches, top 4 toasted bread slices or roll bottoms with the steak, dividing it evenly, then pile the sprout salad on top. Close with the remaining bread slices or roll tops and cut each sandwich in half. Serve immediately.

Makes 4 sandwiches

1½–2 lb flank steak

2–3 tablespoons soy sauce

8 slices good bread or 4 rolls, split (I like peasant bread or crusty sesame rolls)

3 cups thinly sliced Brussels sprouts

FOR THE DRESSING

Juice of 1 lemon

1 clove garlic, grated

2 tablespoons mayonnaise

2 teaspoons Dijon mustard

½ cup olive oil

2–3 tablespoons grated Parmesan cheese

Kosher salt and freshly cracked black pepper

Rib Eye with Campfire Horseradish Mashed Potatoes

I don't grill my steaks directly on the grate. To me, it's a job for a cast-iron frying pan. I want my steak to cook in its own juices, and then I want to pour those juices over the top of my steak before serving. I don't want to lose any of that fat or flavor. So if you've been grilling your steaks on the grate, I urge you to try it this way instead.

While you have the fire going, make the most of it by throwing a few potatoes into the coals. Cooking potatoes this way and taking a few extra steps to make horseradish mashed potatoes is absolutely worth it.

To prepare the potatoes, build a campfire and allow it to burn until the logs become pieces of charcoal and there is ash on the bottom of the firepit. Using tongs, carefully place the potatoes in the embers but not directly in the flames. Allow them to cook for about 30 minutes and then flip them to cook for another 30 minutes, keeping an eye on them to make sure they're exposed to heat without catching fire.

While the potatoes cook, allow the steak to come to room temperature. Salt it generously on both sides at least 10 minutes before you begin to cook it.

Set your cast-iron frying pan on the grate over the fire and heat to medium-high. When the pan is ripping hot, add the steak and cook until it forms a deeply browned crust on the first side, about 6 minutes. Using tongs, flip the steak and add the thyme and butter to the pan. As soon as the butter melts, tip the pan slightly so all the butter pools to one side, then spoon the butter up and over the steak to baste it. Cook until a deeply browned crust forms on the second side, 1–2 minutes. Use your instant-read thermometer to test the internal temperature of the steak; it should register 130°–135°F for medium rare or until done to your liking. Transfer to a cutting board and let rest for 10 minutes. Set the pan with the butter, juices, and thyme aside.

While the steak is resting, retrieve your potatoes from the fire, break them open, and carefully scoop out all the fluffy flesh into a large bowl. Season the potato flesh with salt and pepper. Then begin to add the milk, about ½ cup at a time, while breaking up the potatoes with a large fork. Mix the milk in thoroughly with the fork. Add the butter, chives, horseradish, and sour cream and mash the potatoes until the desired creaminess is reached, adding more sour cream if needed. Taste and adjust with salt and pepper. Cover to keep warm until serving.

Cut the rib eye into thin slices against the grain and transfer to a platter. Pour the contents of the pan over the top. Serve immediately with the mashed potatoes.

Makes 2 servings

FOR THE POTATOES

8 Yukon gold potatoes (about 2 lb)

Kosher salt and freshly cracked black pepper

1 cup whole milk

½ cup (1 stick) butter, softened

1 small bunch fresh chives, chopped

1 tablespoon prepared horseradish

¼ cup sour cream, plus more as needed

FOR THE STEAK

1 bone-in rib eye steak, about 12 oz

Kosher salt and freshly cracked black pepper

1 small bunch fresh thyme

1–2 tablespoons butter

one-pot meals

Challenging myself to cook an entire meal in one pot or pan has been a road full of surprises. Things I'd never tried before proved to be incredibly useful tricks with delicious results. As I worked to keep everything in one vessel, I realized how much sense it made and how many unnecessary dishes I was dirtying in the past. This mentality is crucial in a tiny kitchen, but I know that I'll be taking these practices with me to not-so-tiny cooking spaces in my future. This approach became less about restriction and more about efficiency.

Cast-Iron Chorizo Nachos

This is party food. It's what you want to make when you're having a couple of buds over and you don't want to get distracted by cooking. You're sort of just mixing things, cooking a few components all in the same pan, and then just melting some cheese. It's both easy peasy and a crowd-pleaser, and it must be served with a crisp Mexican beer like Tecate or Modelo plus lime.

Prepare a charcoal or gas grill for direct cooking over medium-high heat. Or light a campfire and place a grate over a section of the firepit with medium-high heat.

Set a large cast-iron frying pan on the grill or campfire grate. When the pan is hot, add the chorizo and cook, breaking it up with the back of a wooden spoon, until golden and crispy on all sides, about 5 minutes. Transfer to a bowl.

Layer the tortilla chips, then cheese, and then beans (if using) into the pan. Top evenly with the chorizo and cover the pan with aluminum foil. Cook until the cheese has melted, about 10 minutes.

Take the pan off the fire and remove the cover. Top with the avocado, cilantro, and jalapeños, drizzle with hot sauce, and finish with a big squeeze or two of lime. Serve immediately.

Makes 4 servings

1 lb Mexican chorizo, casings removed

1 bag (11–12 oz) large, sturdy tortilla chips

3–4 cups shredded pepper jack cheese

1 can (15 oz) refried beans (optional)

2 avocados, halved, pitted, peeled, and sliced

¼ cup fresh cilantro leaves, chopped

1 can (11–12 oz) pickled jalapeños with carrots, drained

Hot sauce for drizzling

1 lime, halved

Scallops with Peas and Prosciutto

This recipe is so funny to me. Every time I came across it while working on this book, I would smile and think, "What are you doing here? You're far too elegant for a camper cookbook. How did you sneak in among the beans and pancakes?" It's here because I'm in love with scallops, and they're almost always a one-pan cooking experience. Just because something is typically seen at high-end restaurants doesn't mean it won't work in an exceptional way over a campfire. I have a wonderful local market that offers beautiful scallops, so if they're available to me, why not indulge?

Place a rack on a sheet pan and set it near the stove. Heat a large cast-iron frying pan over medium-high heat. When the pan is hot, add the prosciutto and cook like bacon, flipping to get both sides, until the fat has rendered out and each slice is as crispy as possible, 3–5 minutes. Transfer the prosciutto to the rack so it remains crisp, leaving the fat behind in the pan.

If the pan is not evenly coated with prosciutto fat, add a little oil. Add the scallops and sear until a golden crust forms on the underside, then flip to form the same crust on the other side. This should take only a minute or two on each side; if left too long, the scallops will overcook and be chewy. Once they are properly seared on both sides, transfer them to a plate, cover with aluminum foil to keep warm, and set aside.

Add more oil if needed to coat the bottom of the pan, then add the shallots and cook, stirring occasionally, until they have softened and are browning, 5–7 minutes. Pour in the wine and deglaze the pan, stirring to dislodge any browned bits on the pan bottom.

Add the peas and stir, then add the lemon zest, season with kosher salt and pepper, and cook until the peas are vibrant green, 1–3 minutes. Pour the peas out onto a large platter and place the scallops on top of the peas.

Add the butter and lemon juice to the pan and swirl the pan until the butter melts. Pour the lemon butter over the scallops and peas, then crumble the prosciutto over the top. Finish with flaky salt and more pepper and serve immediately.

Makes 2 servings

2–4 slices prosciutto

Olive oil for cooking if needed

10 large scallops

2 shallots, thinly sliced

1 cup dry white wine

2 cups shelled English peas (fresh or thawed frozen)

Grated zest and juice of 1 lemon

Kosher salt and freshly cracked black pepper

1 tablespoon butter

Flaky salt for finishing

Garlicky Beans and Escarole

I couldn't imagine a camper cookbook without a recipe like this: a big pile of brothy beans and wilted greens mixed with bits of salty, fatty meat, crispy bread crumbs, and gooey Parmesan. You don't really need anything else because it's a whole meal in a bowl. Feel free to use kale or spinach or whatever leafy green you have, but if you can get your hands on escarole, it's the ideal green for this pot. Also, you can use more or less liquid, depending on whether you prefer a soupy dish or a sautéed pile of beans and greens. Eat as a side dish or the main course at dinnertime or top with a couple of fried eggs for a lovely little breakfast.

Place a Dutch oven over medium-high heat. When the pot is hot, coat the bottom with oil. When the oil is shimmering, add the bread and cook until golden and toasty on the underside, then stir and continue to cook, stirring often, until each piece is golden and crispy, about 10 minutes. Transfer the bread to a small bowl, season with salt and pepper, and set aside.

Add the salami to the pot and cook, stirring frequently, until the fat has rendered out, about 5 minutes. Add the shallots and cook them in the rendered fat, stirring often, until tender, about 3 minutes. Add the beans and escarole and cook, stirring frequently, until the escarole has wilted, about 10 minutes.

Add the bouillon base and water, adjusting the amount according to how soupy you want the dish, then stir well, cover, reduce the heat to a simmer, and cook for 10 minutes. Uncover, stir well, add the Parmesan, garlic, and lemon juice, and season with salt and pepper. Allow to simmer uncovered for a few minutes to melt the cheese and blend the flavors.

Remove from the heat, top with the toasted bread and more Parmesan, and serve directly from the pot.

Makes 4–6 servings

Olive oil for cooking

1½ cups torn sourdough bread, in small pieces

Kosher salt and freshly cracked black pepper

2 oz salami, bacon, or pancetta, diced

2 shallots, thinly sliced

2 cans (15 oz each) cannellini beans, drained

1 head escarole, chopped

1 tablespoon Better Than Bouillon seasoned vegetable base

2 cups water (feel free to add more for a soupier consistency)

¼ cup grated Parmesan cheese, plus more for finishing

4 cloves garlic, grated

Juice of 1 lemon

Kapusta Grilled Cheese

Kapusta can mean a few different things in Polish, but for our purposes, it's cabbage or sauerkraut fried or braised with some sort of fat (bacon, butter, or kielbasa), and it's one of my favorite Polish dishes, right up there with pierogies and stuffed cabbage. I love it on its own, but it makes a really special grilled cheese.

Heat a large cast-iron frying pan over medium-high heat. When the pan is hot, add the bacon and cook, stirring occasionally, until crispy, about 5 minutes. Transfer the bacon to a plate or bowl, leaving the rendered fat in the pan.

Add the sauerkraut to the pan and fry it in the bacon fat, stirring frequently, until it browns and its liquid has evaporated, 3–5 minutes. Return the bacon to the pan, then add the tomato paste, stir to coat the sauerkraut, and cook, stirring often, to blend the flavors, 1–2 minutes. Transfer the sauerkraut to the plate used for the bacon.

Reduce the heat to medium and melt the butter in the pan, tipping the pan to coat the bottom evenly. Lay 2 slices of the bread in the pan side by side and top each one with 2 slices of the cheese and half of the sauerkraut mixture. Place the remaining 2 bread slices on top of the sauerkraut. Griddle the sandwiches, gently flipping them once, until the bread on both sides is deep golden brown and the cheese is fully melted, 1–3 minutes on each side.

Transfer the sandwiches to plates, cut them in half, and serve immediately.

Makes 2 servings

3 slices bacon, chopped

2 cups well-drained sauerkraut

2 tablespoons tomato paste or ketchup

2 tablespoons butter

4 large slices sourdough or peasant bread

4 slices sharp Cheddar cheese

Camper's Soup

This soup starts with leftovers, which feels resourceful. Like many of my recipes, this isn't one you'll have to stick to exactly. It's more about following the process and using what you have on hand. If you're camping for multiple evenings and find yourself with some leftovers from a smoky barbecue dinner, you can use all that flavor to power this soup. Start with your leftover meat. I usually use chicken or chicken legs. Put the bones in, too, then fish them out once the stew base is done.

You don't have leftover grilled meats but still wanna make this recipe? There are a ton of grocery-store options. A smoked turkey leg, smoked pork shoulder, smoked ham, or smoked chicken will create the flavor you're looking for here.

Light your campfire.

When the coals are hot, place a cast-iron Dutch oven directly on the coals in your firepit. When the pot is hot, add the meat and bones and cook, stirring occasionally, for about 5 minutes. Add the carrots, celery, and onion and cook, stirring occasionally, until the vegetables are tender, about 10 minutes. Season with salt and pepper, then add the tomatoes, stir well, and cook, stirring every now and then, for about 10 minutes. Add the water, adjusting the amount according to how thick you want the soup, and the bouillon base. Stir well, cover, and simmer undisturbed for about 1 hour.

Uncover the pot and, using tongs, remove and discard the bones. Add the orzo, stir well, and cook, stirring occasionally, until the orzo is tender, about 10 minutes. (If the orzo absorbs too much liquid, just add a bit more water to the pot.) Stir in the basil, oregano, garlic, vinegar, and Parmesan and simmer, stirring occasionally, for about 15 more minutes to blend the flavors.

Season with salt and pepper, finish with the lemon juice and more Parmesan, and serve immediately.

Makes about 8 servings

About 2 cups cut-up grilled meat, with the bones

3 large carrots, sliced

3 celery ribs, sliced

1 large white onion, chopped

Kosher salt and freshly cracked black pepper

1 can (28 oz) crushed tomatoes

2–4 cups water

1–2 tablespoons Better Than Bouillon seasoned vegetable base

2 cups orzo

1 cup chopped fresh basil

1 tablespoon chopped fresh oregano

2 cloves garlic, grated

Splash of red wine vinegar

1 cup grated Parmesan cheese, plus more for finishing

Juice of 1 lemon

White Bean and Kale Galette

This easy, hearty vegetarian meal is a perfect example of why it's always a good idea to have some puff pastry ready to go in your freezer. I love serving this as a main dish, accompanied with a bright and citrusy salad, or treating it as a side dish along with some seared sausages. Either way, it's always a lovely thing to bring to the table. Like the Lamb and Fennel Pie on page 97, this recipe cheats a bit by using both a frying pan and a sheet pan, but it's simple to execute.

Place a Dutch oven over medium heat. When the pot is hot, coat the bottom with oil. When the oil is shimmering, add the onion and cook, stirring often, until tender, 3–5 minutes. Add the sage and continue to cook, stirring often, until the onion is browned, 2–4 minutes. Pour in the wine and deglaze the pot, stirring to dislodge any browned bits from the pot bottom.

Add the kale and cook, stirring, until wilted, about 5 minutes, adding more oil if needed to prevent sticking. Add the beans, Parmesan, garlic, and lemon zest and juice, season with salt and pepper, and stir well. Cook, stirring frequently, until the beans are just starting to fall apart, 5–10 minutes. Remove from the heat.

While the vegetables are cooking, preheat the oven to 400°F. Line a sheet pan with parchment paper.

Lay the puff pastry flat on the parchment-lined pan. Spoon the bean and kale mixture onto the center of the pastry, leaving about a 3-inch border. Fold the border up over the filling, forming loose pleats around the edges and leaving the center open.

Bake the galette until the pastry is golden brown, about 30 minutes. Let cool for about 10 minutes, then slice and eat!

Makes 4 servings

Olive oil for cooking

1 white onion, sliced

5 fresh sage leaves, chopped

½ cup dry white wine

2–3 cups stemmed and torn kale leaves

1 can (15 oz) cannellini beans, drained and rinsed

½ cup grated Parmesan cheese

2 cloves garlic, grated

Grated zest and juice of 1 lemon

Kosher salt and freshly cracked black pepper

1 sheet puff pastry dough, about 10 × 10 inches, thawed according to package directions

Creamy Artichoke and Caper Soup

This soup is a miracle. It calls for no dairy, but it is wonderfully creamy, thanks to the ultra-velvety texture of the Yukon gold potatoes. Although it looks like any other puréed soup that might taste a little bland or boring, this one surprises you with its bold flavor. Rich, filling, bright, and briny, it's a soup that works for any meal, any time of the year. Serve it with lots of crusty bread and butter or top it with homemade toasted croutons or bread crumbs.

Place a Dutch oven over medium-high heat. When the pot is hot, coat the bottom with oil. When the oil is shimmering, add the shallots and cook, stirring often, until tender, 5–10 minutes. Add the artichokes and their liquid and cook, stirring occasionally, until they begin to break up a bit and the liquid is reduced by about half, 10–15 minutes. Add the capers, stir well, and continue to cook, stirring occasionally, until the liquid has reduced by about half again, 10–15 minutes.

Pour in the wine and deglaze the pan, stirring to dislodge any browned bits from the pot bottom. Season with salt and pepper and cook, stirring occasionally, for about 10 minutes.

Add the water and bouillon base, stir well, and bring to a boil. Add the potatoes, cover the pot, reduce the heat to medium-low, and cook until the potato cubes are tender and beginning to fall apart, about 20 minutes.

Remove from the heat and add the spinach, if using. Using an immersion blender, blend the soup until smooth. Taste and season with salt and pepper if needed. Serve immediately.

Makes 6–8 servings

Olive oil for cooking

2 shallots, thinly sliced

2 jars (12 oz each) marinated artichokes

3 tablespoons capers, drained

½ cup dry white wine

Kosher salt and freshly cracked black pepper

6 cups water

1 heaping tablespoon Better Than Bouillon seasoned vegetable base

4 large Yukon gold potatoes, cut into small cubes

1 cup fresh spinach leaves (optional)

Lamb and Fennel Pie

This isn't technically a one-pot recipe. Yes, everything is cooked together in a cast-iron frying pan, but then it's all tucked into a buttery puff pastry crust inside a pie pan. So, yeah, that's two pans, and I'm really sorry for that, but if you make this pie, I think you'll be able to forgive me. There is nothing in this world cozier than a savory pie, and this one is just so special. It doesn't matter how old or banged-up your oven is. The pie will still bake up crispy and golden brown. If my oven can do it, so can yours. Serve this perfect pie with a nice green salad with a bright dressing to balance out all that incredible lamb fat.

Heat a large cast-iron frying pan over medium-high heat. When the pan is hot, add the lamb and cook, stirring and breaking up the meat with the back of a wooden spoon, until it is crisp and browned but still a little pink, about 5 minutes (do not add salt). Transfer the lamb to a large bowl, leaving the rendered fat in the pan.

If the pan bottom is not evenly coated with fat, add a tablespoon or two of oil. Add the tomato paste and stir, then add the fennel and shallots and stir to coat them with the fat. Add the paprika, season with salt and pepper, and stir well. Cook, stirring often, until the fennel and shallots are browned and very tender, 10–15 minutes.

Add the vinegar and deglaze the pan, stirring to dislodge any browned bits from the pan bottom, then stir in the peas. Stir everything together once more, then add the vegetable mixture to the bowl containing the lamb. Stir until the lamb and vegetables are well mixed, and set aside.

Preheat the oven to 400°F.

Lay a sheet of puff pastry in a 9-inch pie pan, gently pressing it against the bottom and up the sides of the pan with your fingers. Pour the lamb-vegetable mixture into the lined pan and spread it evenly. Gently lay the second sheet of puff pastry on top of the pan, trim away any excess, and then, using your fingers, firmly crimp together the edges of the sheets around the rim of the pan. With a sharp knife, slit a roughly 2-inch X in the center of the pie (for steam to escape).

Bake the pie until the pastry puffs and is crisp and golden, about 20 minutes. Let cool for about 10 minutes before slicing and serving.

Makes 6 servings

1 lb ground lamb

Olive oil for cooking if needed

2 teaspoons tomato paste

1 small fennel bulb, thinly sliced, including fronds

2 shallots, thinly sliced

2 teaspoons smoked paprika

Kosher salt and freshly cracked black pepper

Splash of red wine vinegar

½ cup frozen English peas, thawed

2 packages (14 oz each) Dufour puff pastry dough, thawed according to package directions

Cabbage Dill Soup

My dad made this soup a lot at the restaurant when I was growing up. I'd have two bowls of it during my shift and then I always took one more home. The combination of cabbage, tomato, dill, and lemon is so Polish and so Greek at the same time—a great representation of both of my parents—so it always tastes like home. It's cozy and comforting but also bright and punchy. And just like most soups, it tastes even better the next day and the day after that. I don't like having huge batches of food that take up space in the camper, but this soup goes quickly, which makes it an exception. Serve it with a big ol' hunk of crusty bread or with rice.

Place a Dutch oven over medium-high heat. When the pot is hot, coat the bottom with oil. When the oil is shimmering, add the onion, carrot, celery, and garlic and cook, stirring often, until the vegetables begin to sweat, 5–7 minutes. Add the cabbage, season with salt and pepper, and stir well. Cover and cook until the cabbage has wilted, about 5 minutes.

Set aside some of the dill for garnish, then add the remainder to the cabbage and stir. Continue to cook, uncovered, until the cabbage is tender and some has browned, about 10 minutes. Add the tomatoes and vinegar, stir well, and then cover, adjust the heat to maintain a simmer, and cook for 20 minutes.

Uncover and pour in the stock, adjusting the amount according to how thick you want the soup. Add the butter, season with salt, and stir. Re-cover and continue to simmer for about 2 hours to blend and deepen the flavor.

Just before serving, squeeze the juice of 1 lemon into the soup and stir. Ladle into bowls, add a little more lemon juice, and then garnish with the reserved dill. Serve at once.

Makes 8–10 servings

Olive oil for cooking

1 large white onion, diced

1 large carrot, sliced

3 celery ribs, chopped

4 large cloves garlic, smashed

1 head savoy cabbage, cored and sliced into wide ribbons

Kosher salt and freshly cracked black pepper

1 bunch fresh dill, chopped

1 can (16 oz) crushed tomatoes

3 tablespoons red wine vinegar

4–8 cups chicken stock

3 tablespoons butter

1–2 lemons, halved

Grated Butternut Squash with Orzo and Dill Sauce

Rockaway, Queens, has some of the most memorable food I've ever eaten. It's the home of my favorite New York slice, at New Park Pizza, my favorite piña colada, at Connolly's (not a food but still must be mentioned), and, of course, Uma's: a restaurant serving Uzbec food that is very dear to my heart.

My favorite thing on the menu, hands down, is the squash manti. Those dumplings, filled with grated butternut squash, onion, and a ton of butter, were out of this world, and I still crave them constantly. Leaving the city, I missed being able to get them regularly, but making dumplings from scratch in a tiny camper seemed like an absolute nightmare. So I made my own version. While it's not a dumpling, I do use the same flavors—grated squash and plenty of onion and butter—and instead of the dough, there's orzo. When I eat this orzo dish, I close my eyes and I almost kinda, sorta feel like I'm at Uma's again after a day of surfing at Rockaway Beach.

To make the sauce, in a small bowl, whisk together the yogurt, vinegar, and dill with a fork, mixing well. Season with salt and pepper. Set aside.

Heat a cast-iron frying pan over medium-high heat. When the pan is hot, coat the bottom with oil. When the oil is shimmering, add the onion and cook, stirring occasionally, until the onion is golden and crispy, 10–15 minutes. Add the squash and cook, stirring often, until very tender, about 10 minutes longer.

Add the orzo and stir to combine. Season with salt and pepper, then stir in the butter. Cook, stirring occasionally, for about 5 more minutes, to heat through and blend the flavors. Taste and season with more salt and pepper if needed.

Transfer the orzo mixture to a serving bowl. Serve immediately with the yogurt sauce spooned on top or in a small bowl on the side.

Makes 4 servings

FOR THE SAUCE

1 cup plain full-fat Greek yogurt

1 tablespoon red wine vinegar

2 tablespoons chopped fresh dill

Kosher salt and freshly cracked black pepper

Olive oil for cooking

1 large white onion, diced

1 small butternut squash, halved, seeded, peeled, and grated

2–3 cups cooked orzo, cooked according to package directions

2 tablespoons butter

Kosher salt and freshly cracked black pepper

Campfire Whole Roast Chicken with Couscous and Calabrian Chile Paste

A cast-iron Dutch oven is a wonderful thing. Before I knew better, I thought it was just a big cauldron for soups and stews. But it's more like a little oven, and it happens to turn out a perfectly roasted chicken. This recipe is spicy, lemony, and fun to make. I like to serve it right out of the pot.

Pat the chicken dry with a paper towel, season it generously with salt and pepper, and let come to room temperature.

Meanwhile, light your campfire. When the fire is ready, nestle a cast-iron Dutch oven in the hot coals in the firepit and heat to medium-high heat.

When the chicken is at room temperature, rub it generously with the chile paste and place it, breast side down, into the pot. Allow it to cook, undisturbed, until the skin on the breast is browned and crispy. This will take 5–15 minutes, depending on the heat of the pot.

Remove the chicken from the pot and set aside on a plate. Add the onions and artichokes to the pot and stir to mix. Push them into an even layer on the bottom and sprinkle with salt and pepper. Place the chicken, breast side up, on top of the vegetables. Cover the pot with its lid, pile hot coals on top of the lid, and allow the chicken to cook undisturbed for about 1 hour.

After an hour, uncover the pot, add the couscous and water around the chicken, re-cover again (but without the coals), and cook until the couscous has absorbed the water and is tender and an instant-read thermometer inserted into the thickest part of a chicken thigh, away from bone, registers 165°F.

Remove the lid, remove the pot from the fire, and let everything rest for 5-10 minutes. Top with the lemon zest and juice, sprinkle with the parsley, and serve.

Makes about 4 servings

1 whole chicken, about 3 lb

Kosher salt and freshly cracked black pepper

2–3 tablespoons Calabrian chile paste

2 large white onions, sliced

1 can (15 oz) artichokes in water, drained

1 cup instant couscous

1 cup water

Grated zest and juice of 2 lemons

¼ cup chopped fresh flat-leaf parsley for finishing

open-fire projects

Not all of my camp recipes are quick and easy. I actually think the most exciting meals are the ones you slow down for. These projects take time and require your full attention. They are the meals that consume you the way a little kid plays a game of flashlight tag. The outside world sort of disappears, and your worries melt away with it. It's just you and the fire and the food and your friends. You're fully focused on the task at hand. Recipes like these combat stress. They are the most beautiful distraction, as you find yourself watching the skin on chicken brown over time, keeping tabs on the internal temperature of a rack of ribs, going out to forage for a wild ingredient with a short harvest season, and keeping your fire alive long enough to braise a big piece of meat. To me, all of these force you to be in the present, like forms of meditation.

Five-Spice Pork Ribs

The first time we made these ribs was in the dead of winter. There was about a foot of snow on the ground, and it was pretty uncomfortable to be outside. So we threw on all our snowboarding gear and broke out some booze to keep warm. I'm a summer girl, but there's something about sitting around a fire with an ice-cold nose that makes the food you're preparing particularly special. It makes the reward of dinner that much sweeter when you're suffering a bit. In this case, the reward is a perfectly juicy, perfectly seasoned, and perfectly cooked rack of ribs.

Pat the rib rack dry with a paper towel and let come to room temperature. In a small bowl, stir together the five-spice powder, salt, and sugar. Coat the whole rib rack with the spice mixture.

While the ribs are coming to room temperature, light your campfire, building the fire over the entire firepit and then pushing the hot coals to one side of the pit and placing the grate over the other side so it isn't getting direct heat.

Place the rib rack on the grate and cook, flipping occasionally, for 3–4 hours. The ribs should never exceed 200°F. Test with an instant-read thermometer, inserting it into the flesh away from bone.

Meanwhile, make the sauce. In a small bowl, whisk together all the ingredients with a fork until the syrup dissolves, then set aside.

Once the internal temperature of the ribs registers 190°–200°F, carefully push the very hot embers under the grill grate so the ribs are cooking over medium-high heat. Brush both sides of the rack with the sauce. Continue to grill, turning once, until the sauce is caramelized and the rack is slightly charred on both sides, 3–5 minutes.

Transfer the rack to a cutting board and let rest for about 5 minutes. Cut the ribs apart, sprinkle with the green onions, and serve.

Makes 4 servings

1 whole rack baby back pork ribs (3½–4 lb)

1 tablespoon five-spice powder

1 tablespoon kosher salt

1 tablespoon sugar

FOR THE SAUCE

½ cup soy sauce

½ cup pure maple syrup

1 tablespoon peeled and grated fresh ginger

1 tablespoon grated garlic

3 green onions, thinly sliced, for garnish

Grilled Lamb and Cucumber Salad Sandwiches

This lamb, of course, will not have any mint jelly for serving. This is Greek lamb, the kind I grew up eating. The dressing is what my family calls SPOOL (salt, pepper, olive oil, oregano, lemon), and it's what we believe goes best on lamb (it's also very good on chicken, pork, or fish). Typically, a lamb sandwich like this would be slathered in tzatziki, but I like making it with a cucumber salad, keeping the herbs and vegetables separate from the yogurt. That way, with every bite of crusty, savory, fatty lamb, you're getting a bright and crunchy bit of salad. It's a sandwich with exceptional balance.

First, make the cucumber salad so it has ample time to marinate. Combine all the ingredients in a storage container with an airtight lid. Cap tightly and shake everything together until the sugar and salt dissolve. Store in the cooler until the sandwiches are ready.

Let the lamb come to room temperature before grilling, then season generously with salt.

While the lamb is coming to room temperature, light a campfire and place the grate over a section of the firepit with medium-high heat. While the grate is heating, make the SPOOL. In a small bowl, whisk together the oil, lemon juice, oregano, salt, and pepper with a fork.

When the grate is hot, place the lamb on it. Grill, turning once, for about 15 minutes on each side, basting it generously with the SPOOL throughout the grilling process. The lamb is ready when it has developed a nice bark on each side and an instant-read thermometer inserted into the thickest part registers 130°–135°F for medium-rare. If you prefer your lamb medium or medium-well, shoot for 140°–145°F.

Transfer the lamb to a cutting board and let rest for 5–10 minutes.

While the meat is resting, slice the bread loaf horizontally almost all the way through, leaving it attached on one side. Drizzle the cut sides with oil, place the loaf cut side down on the grate, and grill until nicely charred, 1–2 minutes. Transfer to the cutting board.

Once the lamb has rested, slice it against the grain as thinly as you can. You will have a bit more lamb than you need for the sandwiches. Cut only what you need and store the rest in an airtight container in the cooler or refrigerator to use for lunch the following day. Squeeze the juice from the lemon halves over the lamb.

To assemble the sandwiches, spread the yogurt in a generous layer on the bottom half of the bread. Arrange the lamb slices on the yogurt, top with a generous layer of cucumber salad, and finish with the dill. Close the top half of the bread over the dill and press down on the top. Then, using a serrated knife, carefully slice the loaf crosswise into thirds or quarters and enjoy.

Makes 3–4 sandwiches

FOR THE CUCUMBER SALAD

1 English cucumber, thinly sliced

½ small red onion, thinly sliced

2 tablespoons rice vinegar

1 teaspoon sugar

1 teaspoon kosher salt

1 butterflied leg of lamb, 2½–3 lb

Kosher salt

FOR THE SPOOL

3 tablespoons olive oil, plus more for the bread

Juice of 1 lemon

3 tablespoons fresh oregano

Kosher salt

1 teaspoon freshly cracked black pepper

1 loaf good Italian bread with sesame seeds

1 lemon, halved

½ cup plain full-fat Greek yogurt

⅓ cup fresh dill, chopped

Sumac-Rubbed Chicken Wings with Charred Green Onion Dipping Sauce

There are few things better on the grill than chicken wings. They hold so much fat because they're mostly skin, so I find it difficult to overcook them. These are particularly tasty because of the sumac, which has a beautiful citrusy, floral flavor. I grill the wings coated in a dry rub and then brush them with a mixture of honey and hot sauce to make them sticky, sweet, and spicy. But to be honest, they are really lovely without the sauce if you want to simplify the process and just use the sumac dry rub. Either way, they are really fun to make and eat.

Place the chicken wings on a sheet pan and pat them dry with a paper towel. Let them sit out to dry a bit and come to room temperature while you light a grill or campfire and make the dipping sauce.

Prepare your charcoal or gas grill for direct cooking over medium heat. Or light a campfire and place a grate over a section of the firepit with medium heat.

When the grate is hot, make the dipping sauce. Place the green onions on the grate and grill, rotating them with tongs, until soft and charred on the outside. This should take only about 5 minutes. Transfer the onions to a cutting board, let cool, and then chop finely.

In a small bowl, whisk together the charred onions, buttermilk, sour cream, lemon zest and juice, oil, vinegar, and onion powder with a fork. Season with salt and pepper. Set the dipping sauce aside in your cooler or refrigerator.

In another small bowl, whisk together the sumac, salt, onion powder, and sugar with a fork. Coat the chicken wings evenly with the spice mixture. Rinse and dry the bowl, then add the honey and hot sauce and whisk together with a fork. Set aside for basting.

Place the chicken wings on the grate and cook attentively, rotating them and moving them around with tongs as needed to color evenly. Allow them to cook for about 15 minutes, at which point they should have a bit of char, then generously brush them with the honey mixture. Once the wings are fully coated, grill them, turning as needed, until the sauce has caramelized, 10–15 minutes longer. The wings should take a total of 25–30 minutes to grill.

When the wings are ready, transfer them to a platter and serve right away with the dipping sauce.

Makes 3–4 servings

12 chicken wings

2 tablespoons ground sumac

1 tablespoon kosher salt

1 tablespoon onion powder

1 tablespoon sugar

½ cup honey

1 tablespoon hot sauce

FOR THE DIPPING SAUCE

3 green onions

½ cup buttermilk

¼ cup sour cream

Grated zest and juice of 1 lemon

1 tablespoon olive oil

1 teaspoon red wine vinegar or white wine vinegar

1 tablespoon onion powder

Kosher salt and freshly cracked black pepper

Whole Stuffed Fish

A whole fish is such an elegant thing to eat, and it's especially memorable when it's cooked over a campfire. I like to use grape leaves as part of the stuffing because you can find them in jars in almost any grocery store and I appreciate anything that mimics the taste of dolmas (Greek-style stuffed grape leaves). I use bread crumbs for this recipe, but I also like using cooked rice or couscous for the stuffing. If you can't find branzino, red snapper and sea bass also work great.

Light a campfire and place a grate over a section of the firepit with medium-high heat.

To make the stuffing, in a small bowl, combine the bread crumbs, grape leaves, dill, basil, lemon zest, half of the lemon juice, and 1 tablespoon of the oil and mix well. Season with salt and pepper.

When the grate is hot, place a large cast-iron frying pan on it. While the pan heats, rub the outside of the fish with 1 tablespoon of the oil and season the fish inside and out with salt and pepper. Stuff the fish cavity with the bread crumb mixture. In a small bowl, stir together the remaining 2 tablespoons oil and remaining lemon juice and season with salt and pepper, then set aside for serving.

When the pan is hot, place the fish in it. Cook, turning once, for 4–8 minutes on each side, depending on the size of your fish. The fish is ready when the flesh is opaque and flakes when tested with a knife tip at the thickest point and the skin is crispy on both sides.

Remove the pan from the grate, sprinkle the fish with a little dill and basil, and serve with the oil-lemon mixture, spooning it over the fish as you eat it.

Makes 1–2 servings

FOR THE STUFFING

½ cup dried bread crumbs

3 jarred grape leaves, finely chopped

1 tablespoon finely chopped fresh dill, plus more for sprinkling

1 tablespoon finely chopped fresh basil, plus more for sprinkling

Grated zest and juice of 1 lemon

4 tablespoons olive oil

1 whole branzino, 1–1¼ lb, scaled and cleaned

Kosher salt and freshly cracked black pepper

Black Vinegar Pork Shoulder

I love Chinese black vinegar right out of the bottle as a dipping sauce, but it's also a fantastic cooking ingredient. This delicious pork is ready for anything. It's wonderful over rice or in a sandwich, but I think the best way to enjoy it is wrapped in a flour tortilla or a scallion pancake with herbs. Definitely make the cabbage slaw to accompany it. I believe that heavy, fatty meats should always be served with something bright, fresh, and acidic to balance them out, and this pork and slaw were made for each other.

Let the pork come to room temperature, then season generously with salt and pepper and the cumin.

While the pork is coming to room temperature, prepare a charcoal or gas grill for direct cooking over medium-high heat. Or light a campfire and place a grate over a section of the firepit with medium-high heat.

Set a Dutch oven on the grill or campfire grate. When the pot is hot, place the pork, fat side down, into it and let cook undisturbed until the bottom is seared and is a deep brown, 5–10 minutes. Using tongs, flip the pork and cook undisturbed on the meat side until seared and deep brown, 3–5 minutes. Add the brown sugar, black and rice vinegars, and soy sauce to the pot, distributing them evenly around the pork. Cover and let the pork simmer in the liquid for 1 hour.

Uncover the pot, flip the pork again with tongs, re-cover, and let simmer for 1 hour longer.

Uncover the pot and, using the tongs and a fork, coarsely shred the meat. Once the whole roast is shredded, give everything in the pot a good stir and allow to simmer, uncovered, for 1 more hour.

While the pork is simmering, make the slaw. In a large bowl, whisk together the vinegar, salt, and sugar with a fork until the salt and sugar dissolve. Add the cabbage and massage the vinegar mixture into the cabbage with your hands until the cabbage is evenly moistened.

When the pork is ready, remove from the grate and serve directly from the pot with the slaw on the side.

Makes 6–8 servings

FOR THE PORK

1 boneless pork shoulder roast, about 3 lb

Kosher salt and freshly cracked black pepper

1 teaspoon ground cumin

½ cup firmly packed light brown sugar

½ cup Chinese black vinegar

¼ cup rice vinegar

¼ cup soy sauce or tamari

2-inch piece fresh ginger, peeled and grated

4 cloves garlic, grated

FOR THE SLAW

½ cup rice vinegar, white or red wine vinegar

1 teaspoon kosher salt

1 teaspoon granulated sugar

1 head savoy cabbage, cored and shredded

Shrimp with Ramp Butter

Every year, ramp season comes around and I feel reborn. Those early spring days when everything is slowly starting to bloom after a long frozen upstate winter, I feel like I can finally drop my shoulders when I walk outside. By the end of winter, my energy is pretty low. I do make time for winter hiking and snowboarding, but for most of the winter, I'm hibernating. When the days grow longer and I don't need a jacket outside, I get this surge of energy. This internal excitement grows because I know summer is coming. That feeling always coincides with ramp season—a short window when Sean and I will roll around in the truck to all our secret ramp foraging spots.

My favorite thing to make with ramps is compound butter to keep in the freezer so we can enjoy the flavor of this wild edible all year long. The butter is outstanding on shrimp but is also great on chicken, beef, pork, fish, and vegetables—almost anything. That's why although the shrimp recipe calls for only ½ cup ramp butter, the butter preparation yields much more, which you can tuck away in the freezer to use in the future. I like making this dish in wintertime, when I'm not feeling my best, because it reminds me of early spring, when everything, including me, comes back to life again.

To make the ramp butter, finely chop the ramps and transfer to a bowl. Add the butter and lemon zest and season with salt and pepper. Mix everything together with a rubber spatula or blend with an immersion blender, making sure the ramps are distributed evenly throughout the butter. Wrap the butter in parchment or waxed paper and store in the fridge. If you'd like to freeze it, slip the paper-wrapped butter into a ziplock bag. The butter will keep in the freezer for up to 1 year.

Prepare a charcoal or gas grill for direct cooking over medium heat. Or light a campfire and place a grate over a section of the firepit with medium heat.

Set a large cast-iron frying pan on the grill or campfire grate. When the pan is hot, coat the bottom with oil. When the oil is shimmering, add the shrimp (depending on the size of your pan, you may have to do this in two batches, adding half each of the shrimp and butter for each batch). Cook the shrimp on the first side until it is vibrant pink, 1–2 minutes. Flip the shrimp, add the ramp butter, and cook until the second side is vibrant pink, 1–2 minutes. Then stir the shrimp with a wooden spoon or tongs to ensure every one of them is well coated with melted butter. Once the butter starts to brown, transfer the shrimp to a platter.

Squeeze the juice from the lemon halves over the shrimp, sprinkle with salt, and serve right away.

Makes 2–4 servings

FOR THE RAMP BUTTER

1 bunch ramps (15–20 ramps), roots trimmed if still attached, then thoroughly rinsed

1 lb good butter, at room temperature (I like Kerrygold brand)

Grated zest of 1 lemon

Flaky salt and freshly cracked black pepper

Olive oil for cooking

2 lb large shrimp in the shell, deveined

½ cup ramp butter

1 lemon, halved

Flaky salt

Two Whole Chickens with Dipping Sauces

This recipe is a group activity—a project to work on with your friends while you drink beers. It's a task that requires teamwork and is about sharing in both the process and the satisfaction of the feast. For Sean and me, it is now a sort of ritual that we carry out with our dear friends Brittany and John.

During the 2020 pandemic, the four of us were quarantined together in their beautiful little house in the woods of the Hudson Valley, far away from all our other loved ones. We spent time outside, watched the news, weathered emotional storms, and drank entirely too much, for weeks. Feeling frightened by the outside world and the severity of our reality, we were comforted and distracted by planning elaborate dinners together. It was during this time that Brittany and I fantasized about making a cookbook together, and now, two years later, we are doing just that, and I'm wiping away tears thinking of that dream coming true.

My life couldn't have been more up in the air at that time, and my friends granted me the ability to feel grounded during such an unstable chapter. I will be forever and ever and ever grateful for that. One day, in the true depths of our quarantine, we decided to embark on a cooking project simply because we wanted something to do. We set up a makeshift rotisserie rig and spit-roasted two whole chickens. For a few hours, the world stopped turning. It was just the four of us, a fridge full of beer, and these two perfect chickens. We became hyper-focused on the fire, the placement of the chickens, when to flip them, which direction the wind was coming from, and what the chickens' temperature was. For those few hours, I forgot about the pandemic and didn't feel the heaviness of the world around me.

Cooking these chickens does require a little bit of engineering, but I assure you it's worth it. You'll need two iron rods, each 4 feet long and ½–¾ inch in diameter (about eighteen dollars at the hardware store), and two fairly wide, flat logs, each about 3 feet long and 1 foot wide. Stand the logs up their ends on either side of your firepit and then rest the ends of the iron rods on the tops of the logs. This makes a surprisingly sturdy spit for your chickens. There are several other ways to do this that are way more complex and might work just as well, but I love how simple and primitive this structure is. Once you've engineered your chicken spit and your fire is hot, it's time to cook the birds.

continues on next page

continued from previous page

Pat the chickens dry with a paper towel, then rub them generously with salt, pepper, and oil. Divide the sage and rosemary bunches in half. Set aside half of each bunch to use as a brush for basting. Divide the remaining halves in half again and stuff an equal amount of the sage and rosemary into the cavity of each chicken. Let the chickens come to room temperature. In a small bowl, combine about ½ cup oil and the lemon juice, season with salt and pepper, mix well, and set aside to use for basting.

Light a campfire and get the fire good and hot. You want flames that are large but not tall enough to reach your hanging chickens. You want to cook the chickens slowly with heat, not singe them with full fire exposure. Set up the spit for the chickens as described in the headnote. When your fire is ready, carefully slide a chicken onto each iron rod and rest the ends of the rods on the logs next to the fire. Using the reserved herbs as a brush, coat the chickens with the lemon-oil mixture.

Allow the chickens to cook for about 4 hours, rotating them on the rods (by flipping with tongs) once every hour (so both sides cook evenly) and brushing them with the lemon-oil mixture twice an hour. Be sure to keep an eye on the fire and have a stick or fire poker handy to adjust it as needed so the heat is consistent at all times.

The chickens are ready when an instant-read thermometer inserted into the thickest part of a thigh away from bone registers 165°F. When the chickens are done, using tongs, carefully remove them from the rods and let rest for 10–15 minutes before carving.

While the chickens are resting, prepare the sauces. You will make each one in a small bowl. For the yogurt sauce, whisk together the yogurt, garlic, lemon juice, and oil with a fork and season with salt and pepper. For the green sauce, whisk together the oil, lemon zest and juice, vinegar, and sugar with a fork. Whisk in the herbs, then season with salt and pepper. For the red sauce, whisk together all the ingredients, mixing well.

Carve the chickens, then halve the lemon and squeeze the juice over them. Serve with the sauces.

2 whole chickens, about 3 lb each

Kosher salt and freshly cracked black pepper

Olive oil for rubbing and basting

1 small bunch fresh sage

1 small bunch fresh rosemary

Juice of 1 lemon, plus 1 lemon for finishing

FOR THE YOGURT SAUCE

1 cup plain full-fat Greek yogurt

1 large clove garlic, grated

Juice of ½ lemon

1 tablespoon olive oil

Kosher salt and freshly cracked black pepper

FOR THE GREEN SAUCE

½ cup olive oil

Grated zest and juice of 1 lemon

1 teaspoon red wine vinegar or rice vinegar

Pinch of sugar

1 tablespoon finely chopped fresh dill

1 tablespoon finely chopped fresh cilantro

1 tablespoon finely chopped fresh basil

Kosher salt and freshly cracked black pepper

FOR THE RED SAUCE

½ cup chili crisp

3 tablespoons red wine vinegar or rice vinegar

Pinch of sugar

backpack food

Getting out and enjoying the land we call home is what fills my cup—a hike, a bike ride, a kayaking excursion, a day of fishing, even just a walk up the hill to watch the sunset. The only thing better than being out in nature is being out there with a little something to eat and drink. Nothing excites me more than the anticipation of arriving to the viewpoint or the swim spot. What adds to the excitement is the thought of a tasty sandwich, a flavorful salad, or a salty, crunchy snack to share once the destination is reached.

Sure, trail mix provides the calories you need for a day in the great outdoors, but it always makes me feel disappointed and a little bit sick (I think maybe it's the M&M's). There are so many delicious meals that are backpack friendly. What makes food backpack friendly? For me, it's something that doesn't need to be kept particularly hot or cold and gets better if it sits for a little while—something that will marinate instead of getting soggy. I always pack a cooler bag or an ice pack. That way, if it's really hot and the trek has taken longer than expected, it's nice to know the lunch or snack will still be good.

The key is to know how to pack. I use metal containers with screw tops to ensure nothing will leak. I also find that metal containers with clamp lids work well. The sets of screw-top and clamp-top metal containers I have are nesting, which makes them ideal for camper living. I also like collapsible silicone containers, and I can't recommend them highly enough. They take up barely any storage space and have a reliable seal. I've found these three options to be the most trustworthy.

To pack sandwiches, I use butcher paper and masking tape, usually doubling the paper for extra protection. If you really want to play it safe, a compostable ziplock will do the trick. That's my method and those are my materials. I try to avoid plastic, I rarely use glass, and I'm always pleased with the outcome. Also, leftover butcher paper is a great thing to use to get a fire going post-hike!

For utensils and napkins, I wrap my everyday forks and knives in kitchen towels or linen napkins. Everything has a purpose, and there is no waste. The recipes in this chapter are designed to keep you taken care of. They taste wonderful and are filling and nutritious, but they are all really just side dishes to the main course: Mother Nature.

Salami and Salad Sandwiches

We've all experienced a sandwich that was wrapped up to go and just, well, died in its packaging. What a heartbreaking thing: mayo getting weird and runny, shredded iceberg lettuce losing its crunch, bread absorbing dressing and becoming soggy. I love taking a sandwich along with me, so there are a few rules I follow to ensure my sandwich stays intact on my journey: (1) Only use vegetables that are good when they wilt. Kale, escarole, spinach, and, in this case, arugula are delicious when fresh and crisp from the fridge but are just as lovely when a little wilted. (2) Choose a protein that doesn't get weird if it sits out for a while. Sounds gross but it's a very good point. I like cured meats, like salami, prosciutto, or coppa, and I save sliced turkey or tuna salad for another time. (3) Leakproof bread! I skip the white bread or any sort of sandwich bread and go for a baguette or something with a hearty crust that'll act as a shell and won't get soggy.

In a bowl large enough to toss a small salad, combine the shallot with vinegar and/or lemon juice just to cover. Toss together with your fingers so every piece of shallot is soaking in the acid evenly. Let sit for about 5 minutes. Add the arugula and toss everything together. Add a generous drizzle of oil, season with salt and pepper, and toss again. Scatter the Parmesan on top, toss, and set the salad aside.

Cut the baguette in half crosswise, split each half lengthwise, and place the bottom halves cut side up on a work surface. Line the bottom halves with the salami and then generously pile the arugula salad on top. Close with the top halves.

Wrap each sandwich in butcher paper and secure with masking tape to prevent any dressing leakage.

Makes 2 sandwiches

1 shallot, sliced paper-thin

Vinegar of choice and/or fresh lemon juice as needed to cover

3 cups arugula

Olive oil for drizzling

Flaky salt and freshly cracked black pepper

About ½ cup shaved Parmesan cheese (use a vegetable peeler)

1 baguette

8–12 slices salami

Marinated Mussels

Here is a perfect example of something exciting to take on a hike or bike ride. Maybe an oily tinned shellfish snack getting tossed around in your backpack is a scary thought, but if you carry this one in a tightly sealed screw-top metal container, it'll be smooth sailing all the way to the picnic spot.

In a bowl, whisk together the harissa, lemon zest and juice, garlic, and parsley with a fork. Season with salt and pepper. Add the mussels and their oil of one can (drain the other two) and toss gently until evenly coated with the marinade.

Serve the mussels with potato chips for scooping.

Makes 3 servings

2 teaspoons harissa

Grated zest and juice of 2 lemons

1 clove garlic, grated

2 tablespoons finely chopped fresh flat-leaf parsley

Kosher salt and freshly cracked black pepper

3 cans (4 oz each) mussels in oil (ideally smoked)

Potato chips for serving

Smoked Trout Salad

I love smoked trout salad, and I also love French onion dip, so adding fried onions to a creamy trout salad makes me a very happy camper (wink-wink). Enjoy it as a dip for chips and crudités (endive leaves are wonderful for scooping), or use it traditionally, spread on bread or crackers. It's absolute perfection either way and is such a delicious protein option while you're out on the trail.

Heat a large cast-iron frying pan over medium-high heat. When the pan is hot, coat the bottom with oil. When the oil is shimmering, add the onion and cook, stirring constantly, until browned and crispy, 15–20 minutes. Set the onion aside to cool completely.

In a bowl, whisk together the yogurt, lemon zest and juice, vinegar, and dill with a fork, then season with salt and pepper. Fold in the cooled onion, trout, and just enough oil to create a good consistency.

Pack with an ice pack to keep chilled.

Makes about 4 servings

Olive oil for cooking and mixing

1 large white onion, diced

¼–½ cup plain full-fat Greek yogurt (depending on desired creaminess)

Grated zest and juice of ½ lemon

1 teaspoon white or red wine vinegar

2 tablespoons chopped fresh dill

Kosher salt and freshly cracked black pepper

2 smoked trout fillets (about 4 oz each), flaked into small pieces

Simple Marinated Sardines

Last time I made these, I enjoyed them lakeside on a beautiful, sunny June day for a dear friend's birthday. This is a great quick snack, but it's also just perfect for a picnic with friends—elegant yet easy, light yet filling, and always such a joy to eat. Serve it over some nice bread, over salad greens, or with a bag of potato chips.

In a bowl, whisk together the oil, lemon zest and juice, capers, parsley, and chives with a fork. Season with salt and pepper. Add the sardines to the bowl and gently mix, making sure they are evenly coated with the marinade.

Pack with an ice pack, in a container with a screw top or other secure lid.

Makes about 4 servings

2 tablespoons olive oil

Grated zest and juice of 1 lemon

1 tablespoon capers

1 tablespoon finely chopped fresh flat-leaf parsley

1 tablespoon finely chopped fresh chives

Kosher salt and freshly cracked black pepper

2 cans (4 oz each) sardine fillets in water, drained

Green Orzo Salad

My mom makes a lot of orzo salad. Because she made it so often when I was growing up, you could say I know a thing or two about standing at the fridge late at night and shoveling orzo salad into my mouth. And I've found that it is best when it's less orzo and mostly other stuff. This orzo salad, like the others I've inhaled, gets better and better as it sits, making it a fantastic choice for a picnic.

In a large bowl, combine the orzo, oil, vinegar, lemon zest and juice, olives, shallots, cheese, dill, and mint and stir with a wooden spoon or rubber spatula until all the ingredients are evenly distributed. Season with salt and pepper and stir again.

Pack with an ice pack so it stays chilled.

Makes 6–8 servings

6 cups cooked orzo, cooked according to package directions, at room temperature

3 tablespoons olive oil

1 tablespoon red wine vinegar

Grated zest and juice of 1 lemon

1 cup Castelvetrano olives, pitted and coarsely chopped

½ cup store-bought fried shallots, preferably Maesri brand

6 oz feta cheese, cut into small cubes

½ cup finely chopped fresh dill

½ cup finely chopped fresh mint

Kosher salt and freshly cracked black pepper

Charred Shallot, Leek, and Fennel Dip

This recipe is a result of my lifelong love affair with French onion dip. I'm happy just popping open a can of it from the gas station, but this one is laced with little charred bits that I really love.

Prepare a charcoal or gas grill for direct cooking over medium-high heat, light a campfire and top with a grate over a section of the firepit with medium-high heat, or preheat the oven to 400°F.

Trim off the stalks and fronds from the fennel bulb and set the fronds aside for garnish. Trim off the darker green tops (they are tough) and root end from the leek, then discard the tough outer leaf or two. Peel the shallot. Cut the fennel bulb, leek, and shallot in half lengthwise and rub them on both sides with oil.

Arrange the fennel, leek, and shallot halves on the grill or campfire grate and cook, using tongs to turn as needed, until tender and one side is nicely charred. If using your oven, arrange on a sheet pan and roast until tender and deeply browned (charred) on the bottom. The timing will vary depending on the intensity of the heat, but they should all be ready within about 15 minutes.

Transfer the vegetables to a cutting board and let cool. Chop them into small pieces and drop the pieces into a bowl. Add the yogurt, lemon zest and juice, oil, vinegar, onion powder, and most of the green onions, reserving the remainder for garnish. Mix well and season with kosher salt and pepper.

Pack the dip into your backpack-friendly container, then chop the reserved fennel fronds and sprinkle on top along with the reserved green onions. Finish with some flaky salt, a grind of pepper, and a drizzle of oil. When it's time to eat, serve with potato chips.

Makes 6–8 servings

1 small fennel bulb with fronds

1 leek

1 shallot

2 tablespoons olive oil, plus more for rubbing and finishing

1–2 cups plain full-fat Greek yogurt (depending on desired creaminess)

Grated zest and juice of 1 lemon

Splash of vinegar (red wine, sherry, or whatever kind you have)

1 tablespoon onion powder

3 green onions, thinly sliced

Kosher salt and freshly cracked black pepper

Flaky salt for finishing

Potato chips, crudités, or other dipper of choice for serving

Salady Walnut Pesto Pasta

Typical pasta salad does not excite me. I don't care for canned black olives and big hunks of sun-dried tomatoes mixed into it, and I don't like when it's creamy and sweet. It is a mystery to me why those are the two most popular pasta salad styles—the ones you can always find at a grocery store or deli. I feel weird saying I don't like pasta salad because I love pasta and I love salad. But this one is different, because it's fresh and green and exciting. The kind of pasta salad that makes me really happy.

To make the pesto, in a large jar, combine the basil, garlic, lemon juice, walnuts, Parmesan, and ½ cup oil and blend with an immersion blender until smooth. Add the remaining oil and blend until incorporated into the pesto. Season with salt and pepper.

Place the pasta in a large bowl, and pour the pesto over it, mixing until the pasta is coated. Add the arugula and snap peas and toss to mix well. Taste and season with salt and pepper if needed.

Pack with an ice pack to keep it chilled.

Makes 4–6 servings

FOR THE PESTO

4 cups fresh basil leaves

1 clove garlic, halved

Juice of 1 lemon

¼ cup walnuts

½ cup grated Parmesan cheese

1 cup olive oil

Kosher salt and freshly cracked black pepper

1 lb pasta (something fun and short), cooked according to package directions and brought to room temperature

2 cups chopped arugula

1 cup sugar snap peas, sliced lengthwise

Potato Salad in Grainy Mustard Vinaigrette

My potato salad and pasta salad feelings are the same. To be perfectly frank, I don't want creamy potato salad. I like mustardy, vinegary, bright potato salad. This one is as simple as can be, and honestly, I make it exclusively for days when I know I'm going be doing something fun outside. When you're miles into a bike ride and hunger hits, a healthy portion of potatoes will save your goddamn life. Maybe a beer too. Your choice.

In a large bowl, whisk together the mustard, lemon juice, vinegar, and oil with a fork to make a vinaigrette. Add the parsley, chives, and potatoes and mix until each potato half is coated with the vinaigrette. Season with salt and pepper.

Pack with an ice pack to keep chilled.

Makes 4–5 servings

2 tablespoons grainy mustard

Juice of 1 lemon

1 tablespoon red wine vinegar or rice vinegar

3 tablespoons olive oil

½ cup chopped fresh flat-leaf parsley

½ cup chopped fresh chives

3 lb little potatoes, preboiled, cooled, and halved

Kosher salt and freshly cracked black pepper

Cold Roasted Salmon Salad

Roasted salmon right out of the oven is great, of course, but I am an absolute freak for leftover cold roasted salmon. I'm also a big believer in marinating food after it is cooked instead of before, and this dish is a textbook example of why I feel strongly about it.

Preheat the oven to 300°F. Line a sheet pan with parchment paper.

Lay the salmon on the parchment-lined pan. Coat on both sides with ¼ cup of the oil, then season on both sides with salt and pepper. Roast the salmon until it starts to look opaque, about 20 minutes. Remove the salmon from the oven and let cool for 10–15 minutes.

While the salmon is cooling, in a bowl, combine the remaining ¼ cup oil, the onion, lemon juice, capers, and sugar, season with salt and pepper, and stir to mix.

When the salmon is ready, break it up into large flakes and transfer them to the bowl holding the oil mixture. Add the dill and gently mix everything together so the fish stays in large flakes.

Pack with an ice pack to keep chilled.

Makes 4–8 servings

2 lb skinless salmon fillet

½ cup olive oil

Kosher salt and freshly cracked black pepper

½ red onion, thinly sliced

Juice of 1 lemon

1 tablespoon capers

Pinch of sugar

½ cup finely chopped fresh dill

Burnt Eggplant Spread

Throwing an eggplant on a fire, burning the hell out of it, and turning it into a beautiful, creamy, savory spread feels like a magic trick. This recipe works as a side for nearly any campfire dinner, but I love keeping it in a cooler bag so I can spread it on bread and make a sandwich with lots of crunchy lettuce and bright tomato or just spoon it onto crackers or endive leaves.

Prepare a charcoal or gas grill for direct cooking over medium heat. Or light a campfire and place a grate over a section of the firepit with medium heat.

Place the whole eggplants on the grill or campfire grate and cook, flipping them after 10–15 minutes, until they are completely charred on the outside and creamy and soft all the way through, 20–30 minutes. Remove from the fire and let cool for about 10 minutes.

Scoop out all the flesh into a bowl and discard the skin. Add the garlic, harissa to taste, cilantro, oil, and lemon juice and mix and mash with a fork until thoroughly combined. Pack the mixture into a backpack-friendly container, then finish with more cilantro, a drizzle of oil, a sprinkle of salt, and a grind or two of pepper. Serve with pita for scooping.

Makes 6–8 servings

2 large eggplants

2 cloves garlic, grated

1–2 teaspoons harissa

2 tablespoons finely chopped fresh cilantro, plus more for finishing

1–2 tablespoons olive oil, plus more for finishing

Juice of 1 lemon

Flaky salt and freshly cracked black pepper

Pita, crackers, or crudités for serving

Party Popcorn

I like to season popcorn to taste more like potato chips. **We enjoy this snack late at night watching a movie or out on an adventure. To take it on the road, pack it in a ziplock bag so it stays fresh.**

Heat a cast-iron Dutch oven over medium-high heat. When the pot is hot, coat the bottom with oil and add your popcorn kernels. Cover the pot and listen for the sound of kernels starting to pop. Once they start, hold the pot just over the flame and shake it. Continue to shake until the sound of popping kernels slows to about one pop every 5 seconds, then remove the pot from the heat.

Uncover the pot, add a drizzle of oil, the yeast, paprika, onion powder, and rosemary, and season with salt and pepper. Carefully mix up everything with a large spoon, then taste and adjust with more salt and pepper if needed. Pack as much as you'd like in a ziplock bag to take with you, and store the rest in an airtight container for when you return home.

Makes about 4 quarts

Olive oil for cooking and drizzling

½ cup popcorn kernels

½ cup nutritional yeast

1 tablespoon smoked paprika

1 teaspoon onion powder

1 teaspoon ground dried rosemary or thyme

Kosher salt and freshly cracked black pepper

canteen cocktails

Oh, the pure joy of bringing a boozy bev along with you on an adventure. Having a drink is a special treat that is 100 percent better paired with a sunset or a view of some kind. Whether I am on a mountaintop, in a lake, or tailgating post-snowboarding, a refreshing cocktail is always my favorite drink. And so I have two canteens in my collection of food and drink containers: my water canteen and my cocktail canteen. Having one designated for booze keeps the one for water pure and guarantees an ice-cold (or steamy-hot) cocktail on your outdoor adventure. Each of these batch cocktails is designed to come together in a 1-quart canteen, making them perfect for two to four people to share. If you aren't planning on throwing your drink in a backpack, feel free to use a 32-oz mason jar.

Amaro Sour Spritz

I love using amaro in a sour because of its bitterness. I love how the sugar and maraschino cherries balance it out. I also find that most cocktails have a very obvious season, but this one feels appropriate to drink year-round.

1 cup amaro

2 tablespoons sugar

Ice

Juice of 2 lemons

4 lemon peel strips, each 3 inches long and 1 inch wide

4 fresh mint sprigs

8 Luxardo maraschino cherries

Sparkling water

Add the amaro, sugar, ice, lemon juice, lemon peel, mint, and cherries to a canteen. Cover and shake well. Add the sparkling water to fill and stir briefly. Pour into glasses and serve.

Jam Drink

This is a great little shortcut to a really juicy, fruity cocktail. Muddling fruit feels too involved for camping, but a little dollop of jam is the perfect amount of effort.

1 cup white rum

1–3 tablespoons Stone Fruit Compote (page 187)
or your favorite fruit jam

1 cup homemade or store-bought lemonade

Ice

Add the rum, compote, lemonade, and ice to a canteen. Cover and shake well. Pour into glasses and serve.

Black Currant Spritz

This is the perfect light-and-bright drink for daytime or evening. It's refreshing, crisp, and rich, with the deep flavor of crème de cassis.

1 cup crème de cassis (I love Current Cassis
but any brand you can find will do)

Ice

4 lemon peel strips, each about 3 inches long and 1 inch wide

4 fresh mint sprigs

Sparkling water

Add the crème de cassis, ice, lemon peel, and mint to a canteen. Cover and shake well. To serve, pour into glasses, filling them about halfway, then add the sparkling water to fill, and stir briefly.

Passion Fruit Colada

I love a piña colada. Especially when it's made with Coco López. I first had this passion fruit rendition on a surf trip in Puerto Rico, and now, whenever I'm near the ocean, this is what I want to drink. When Sean and I are at Rockaway Beach we usually grab some passion fruit juice from the grocery store, hit the liquor store for rum, and mix up this cocktail right in the parking lot before hitting the beach.

1 cup white rum

2 cups store-bought passion fruit juice

½ cup Coco López cream of coconut

Juice of 1 lime

Ice

Add the rum, passion fruit juice, cream of coconut, lime juice, and ice to a canteen. Cover and shake well. Pour into glasses and serve.

Hibiscus-Ginger Gin Fizz

A refreshing spiked, sparkling herbal tea for warm days. Feel free to use your favorite tea, but I find hibiscus to be the most delicious.

3 hibiscus tea bags

2 cups boiling water

2-inch piece fresh ginger

1 cup gin

2 tablespoons honey

Juice of 1 lemon

Ice

Sparkling water

Using the tea bags, boiling water, and ginger, make 2 cups of strong hibiscus tea. Discard the tea bags and ginger, let the tea cool, and pour the tea into a canteen. Add the gin, honey, lemon juice, and ice. Cover and shake well. To serve, pour into glasses, filling them about halfway, then add sparkling water to fill, and stir briefly.

salad stuff

Salad. It's my favorite food. I dream about Hudson Valley spring and summer produce all year long: tomatoes with flaky salt, crisp green beans, the absolutely explosive crunch of romaine lettuce, the way any stone fruit tastes with a garlicky vinaigrette, tender herbs when they're sweetly flowering, cucumbers in every shape and size. It's the time of year I'm the happiest, in large part because of the glorious produce.

Deep Summer Panzanella

A salad with a whole loaf of bread in it is a very good salad. Panzanella is a perfect food because it celebrates the magic that happens when bread soaks up salad dressing, and I can never get enough of that experience. This recipe is for late summer, when tomatoes are spot-on and you have more than you know what to do with.

Prepare a charcoal or gas grill for direct cooking over medium heat.

In a large bowl, combine the heirloom and cherry tomatoes, cucumber, dill, basil, and garlic. Sprinkle with the vinegar, season with salt and pepper, and mix gently. Set aside to marinate.

Brush the bread chunks with oil and sprinkle with salt. Place on the grill and grill, turning as needed, until golden brown on all sides and crunchy. Remove the bread from the grill and let it cool almost completely.

Add the bread to the tomato mixture, add the ¼ cup oil, and stir until the bread is evenly coated with juices from the salad. Taste and add more salt and pepper if needed. Serve immediately.

Note: *The easiest way to slice the basil leaves is to pile them in three or four stacks, roll up each stack tightly from a long side, and then cut crosswise into narrow strips.*

Makes 4–6 servings

3 large heirloom tomatoes, chopped

1 pint orange cherry tomatoes (about ¾ lb), halved

1 English cucumber, chopped

½ cup fresh dill, chopped

½ cup fresh basil leaves, sliced into ribbons (see Note)

1 clove garlic, grated

2–4 tablespoons red wine vinegar

Kosher salt and freshly ground black pepper

1 small loaf day-old peasant bread, torn into roughly 2-inch chunks

Olive oil for brushing, plus about ¼ cup for dressing the salad

Big Green Salad with Lemon-Tamari Dressing

When I was growing up, some version of this salad made a regular appearance on our summer dinner table. It reminds me of eating out on the deck with my whole family. My dad is a serious meat eater, and in the summer, he frequently grilled a giant pile of steaks, lamb chops, sausages, burgers, or hot dogs for me, my mom, my big brothers, and usually a few of my brothers' friends. Because the meals were typically so meat-forward, my mom would put together a massive salad, always in a giant wooden bowl, to balance out the menu. Sean is a big meat eater, and when we are cooking over fire, a lot of our meals tend to include meat. So this recipe is still being used to balance out a meat-heavy dinner table.

To make the dressing, in a small bowl, whisk together the tamari, garlic, mustard, and lemon juice with a fork. Then slowly stream in the oil while whisking constantly, adding just enough to create a good dressing consistency. Season with salt and pepper and whisk to mix.

In a large bowl, combine the lettuce, cucumber, radishes, and the microgreens and edible flowers, if using. Pour the dressing over the top and give everything a good toss with a set of tongs. Serve immediately.

Makes 4–6 servings

FOR THE DRESSING

2 tablespoons tamari or soy sauce

1 clove garlic, grated

1 teaspoon Dijon mustard

Juice of 1 lemon

¼–½ cup olive oil

Kosher salt and freshly cracked black pepper

2 large heads lettuce, leaves separated and torn into bite-sized pieces

1 English cucumber, thinly sliced

3 radishes, thinly sliced

Handful of microgreens (optional)

Handful of edible flowers (optional)

Little Gem with Ranch, Crispy Shallots, and Pistachios

The crispiest, crunchiest, chunkiest salad—I just can't get enough Little Gem in my life. This is a peak summertime salad and an absolute must for a barbecue. It is a great addition to most meals and is everything I want in a salad. Serve it with chicken wings, pulled pork, grilled shrimp, or fried chicken, and you'll be pleased.

To make the dressing, in a small bowl, whisk together the buttermilk, sour cream, onion powder, oil, vinegar, and lemon zest and juice with a fork. Season with kosher salt and pepper and whisk to mix.

Arrange the lettuce halves, cut side up, on a large platter. Top with the cucumber slices, squeeze the juice from the lemon half over the vegetables, and then generously pour the dressing over everything. Top with the pistachios, shallots, dill, and chives. Finish with a drizzle of oil, a sprinkle of flaky salt, and a couple of grinds of pepper and serve.

Makes 3–4 servings

FOR THE DRESSING

½ cup buttermilk

¼ cup sour cream

1 tablespoon onion powder

1 tablespoon olive oil

1 teaspoon white or red wine vinegar

Grated zest and juice of 1 lemon

Kosher salt and freshly cracked black pepper

3 heads Little Gem lettuce or romaine hearts, halved lengthwise

2 Persian cucumbers or ½ English cucumber, thinly sliced

½ lemon

½ cup roasted pistachios, chopped

¼ cup store-bought fried shallots, preferably Maesri brand

1 tablespoon chopped fresh dill

1 tablespoon chopped fresh chives

Olive oil for drizzling

Flaky salt and freshly cracked black pepper

Asparagus Salad with Prosciutto and Parmesan

Blanching is perfect for cooking in a tiny space. I love this recipe because it requires only one pot of boiling water. The rest is assembly. You can make this salad any time of year, but I urge you to do it in the springtime, when asparagus is in season. The skinny shoelace ones that are available at the supermarket year-round will work, but the big, chubby asparagus spears from the market in early May are what I'm after. Those guys are absolute magic. And I'm fine with roasted or grilled asparagus, but I don't really understand why most people choose those methods. The stalks just shrivel up and become stringy. To me, enjoying asparagus at its full potential means blanching it until it is just tender. It becomes unctuous and full of flavor, and the color is vibrant. Big, fat, juicy blanched asparagus spears need little else to be the perfect plate of springtime.

Bring a large pot of salted water to a boil over high heat. Drop the asparagus in and boil until just tender and the color is vibrant, about 2 minutes. Drain, rinse under cold water to stop the cooking, and then pat dry.

Arrange the asparagus and prosciutto on a serving plate. Squeeze the juice from the lemon halves over top, then drizzle with the oil and sprinkle with the Parmesan and mint. Finish with salt and pepper and serve.

Makes 2–4 servings

1 bunch thick asparagus, stems trimmed

5 thin slices prosciutto

1 lemon, halved

Olive oil for drizzling

½ cup shaved Parmesan cheese (use a vegetable peeler)

½ cup fresh mint leaves, roughly chopped

Flaky salt and freshly cracked black pepper

Sticky Roasted Carrots with Furikake

Here is another riff on one of my mom's recipes. I love amping up the sweetness of carrots with maple syrup and then balancing it out with a big old bunch of umami from tamari and furikake (see Note). This side dish goes with almost anything, or you can throw it over some rice or a salad because it's equally delicious hot and cold. This is a campfire dish, but the original recipe called for roasting in a 400°F oven because you can also cook it on your camper stove.

Light a campfire and place a grate over a section of the firepit with medium-high heat.

Set a large cast-iron frying pan on the grate. When the pan is hot, add the oil. When the oil is shimmering, add the carrots. Pour the maple syrup and tamari over the carrots and toss with a set of long tongs until the carrots are evenly coated. Cover the pan with its lid and let cook for about 15 minutes. Remove the lid and check on the carrots. If the sauce is caramelized on the bottom, use your tongs to flip the carrots over, then re-cover and cook for another 15 minutes. Watch carefully as the carrots cook to be sure they don't burn.

Uncover the pan and check the carrots again. They should be sticky and caramelized on the outside and tender on the inside. Transfer the carrots and their cooking juices to a serving dish, sprinkle with the furikake, and serve.

Note: *Furikake is a Japanese condiment typically made of dried seaweed, sesame seeds, salt, sugar, and sometimes dried fish. If you don't have furikake on hand, crush some toasted nori and mix it with sesame seeds and flaky salt.*

Makes about 6 servings

2 tablespoons olive oil

5 large carrots, peeled and halved lengthwise

2 tablespoons pure maple syrup

2 tablespoons tamari or soy sauce

½ cup furikake

Plum-Tomato Salad with Salami and Basil

This is more of a guideline than a recipe—a guideline that welcomes switching and swapping of any kind. It should always include some kind of stone fruit, a salty meat, a mellow cheese, a fresh herb, a splash of acid, and a drizzle of good oil. Whatever you can find in these categories will work. For example, the stone fruit that is in season and looks best at the store will be the ideal option. I use plums here, but I also make this salad with peaches, nectarines, cherries, and apricots. Have fun, and although this might sound extremely cliché, let the season guide you.

Arrange the tomato, plums, salami, and mozzarella on a platter. Drizzle generously with the oil and vinegar. Finish with the basil, salt, and a few grinds of pepper and serve.

Makes 2–4 servings

1 large heirloom tomato, cut into large chunks

4 plums, pitted and quartered

¼ lb salami, cut into small chunks

¼ lb fresh mozzarella cheese, cut into small chunks

Olive oil for drizzling

Balsamic vinegar for drizzling

½ cup fresh basil leaves

Flaky salt and freshly cracked black pepper

Grilled Prosciutto-Wrapped Peaches with Burrata and Pesto

Prosciutto and melon? Sure. But prosciutto and peach? That's more my speed. A ripe, in-season peach wrapped in prosciutto and seared on just one side is my favorite thing to eat while sitting around a summer campfire. This recipe creates a wonderful little appetizer situation filled with opportunity to spread and dip and mix and match. But let it be known that if you just squat down next to the fire with your cast-iron pan, slip a couple of thick peach slices wrapped in prosciutto into the pan, leave them until one side is caramelized, and then just pop them into your mouth with absolutely nothing else, it's still a remarkable meal. If you don't feel like lighting a fire, you can also sear them on your camper stove.

Prepare a charcoal or gas grill for direct cooking over medium-high heat. Or light a campfire and place a grate over a section of the firepit with medium-high heat.

Place a large cast-iron frying pan on the grill or campfire grate. While the pan heats, wrap each peach quarter with a ribbon of prosciutto. When the pan is hot, place the wrapped peach quarters in the pan and sear until the undersides are golden and caramelized, 1–2 minutes. Remove from the heat.

Nestle the burrata in the center of the pan with the peaches or arrange on a platter. Gently tear the burrata open. Spoon the pesto over everything, finish with flaky salt, pepper, and basil leaves, and serve.

Makes 4–6 servings

4 ripe peaches, pitted and quartered

8 thin slices prosciutto, torn in half lengthwise

2 large pieces burrata cheese, about 8 oz each

¼–½ cup pesto (see Salady Walnut Pesto Pasta, page 134)

Flaky salt and freshly cracked black pepper

Basil leaves for garnish

Crudités with Creamy Tahini-Tamari Dressing

This dressing is for everything. It's great for crudités but is also an excellent salad dressing (particularly with kale or something very crunchy and sturdy like romaine). I also like it spooned over roasted vegetables, especially sweet potatoes.

In a small bowl, whisk together the tahini, lemon juice, oil, soy sauce, honey, vinegar, onion powder, and chives with a fork. Season with salt and pepper and whisk to mix. Whisk a spoonful of water in at a time until you've achieved your desired consistency.

Arrange your selection of crudités on a platter with the bowl of dressing and serve.

Makes 4–6 servings

½ cup tahini

Juice of 1 lemon

2 tablespoons olive oil

1 tablespoon tamari or soy sauce

1 teaspoon honey

1 teaspoon rice vinegar

1 tablespoon onion powder

1 tablespoon chopped fresh chives

Kosher salt and freshly cracked black pepper

Crudités such as sliced or whole raw carrots, cucumbers, radishes, broccoli, cauliflower, bell peppers, green beans, or asparagus or boiled little potatoes for serving

Radicchio Salad with Pancetta and Breadcrumbs

I love radicchio. I love it because it can be misunderstood and overlooked, but if you treat it the right way, it becomes an obsession. That's how it was for me anyway. When I was younger, I always thought it was so beautiful but way too bitter. As I got older, I realized that to prepare radicchio properly, you have to balance out that bitterness with sweetness and fat. Only then will the radicchio shine. This salad, layered with crispy pancetta and with a generous amount of honey in the dressing, is a great example of that balance. I've made it many times with thinly sliced Gala or Honeycrisp apples instead of pancetta, which is also wonderful and is, of course, vegetarian friendly. This salad is a good reminder that eating giant heaps of crisp vegetables isn't just a summertime thing.

To make the dressing, in a small bowl, whisk together the lemon juice, honey, mustard, vinegar, and thyme with a fork. Slowly stream in the oil while whisking constantly. Season to taste with kosher salt and pepper, whisk to mix, and set aside.

Heat a large cast-iron frying pan over medium-high heat. When the pan is hot, add the pancetta and cook, stirring often, until crispy, 3–5 minutes. Transfer the pancetta to a plate, leaving the fat behind in the pan. Add the bread to the pan and toast, stirring often, until golden brown, 2–4 minutes. Transfer the bread to the plate with the pancetta.

Separate the leaves of each radicchio head and place the whole leaves in a large bowl. Pour the dressing over the radicchio and mix gently with your hands, carefully coating each leaf. Pile the radicchio onto a platter and top with the pancetta, toasted bread, parsley, and Parmesan. Finish with flaky salt and pepper and serve.

Makes 4–6 servings

FOR THE DRESSING

Juice of 1 lemon

1 tablespoon honey

1 teaspoon Dijon mustard

1 teaspoon white or red wine vinegar

1 teaspoon minced fresh thyme

½ cup olive oil

Kosher salt and freshly cracked black pepper

¼-lb piece pancetta, diced

About 1 cup day-old torn bread, in small pieces

2 heads radicchio

Kosher salt and freshly cracked black pepper

Chopped fresh flat-leaf parsley for garnish

⅓ cup grated Parmesan cheese

Flaky salt and freshly cracked black pepper

Raw Corn Salad with Chili Crisp Vinaigrette

Sweet corn is amazingly versatile. It is the star of summer grilling and my personal favorite flavor in any dessert. Plus, there are so many ways to enjoy it: charred, boiled, and on the cob, or as corn pudding, corn chowder, corn fritters, corn bread, and more. This recipe celebrates corn in its truest form. My family regularly included a raw corn salad on the table at summer get-togethers. My version of the warm-weather staple calls for my go-to condiment, chili crisp.

To make the vinaigrette, in a small bowl, whisk together the chili crisp, vinegar, sugar, and lime juice with a fork and set aside.

In a large bowl, combine the corn kernels, cucumber, and green onions and stir with a spoon. Add the lime juice, season with kosher salt and pepper, and toss well.

Pour the corn mixture onto a platter and drizzle the vinaigrette over the top. Garnish with the microgreens, if using, then finish with flaky salt and a grind or two of pepper and serve.

Makes 6–8 servings

FOR THE VINAIGRETTE

½ cup chili crisp

Splash of rice vinegar

Pinch of sugar

Juice of 1 lime

Kernels from 6–8 ears corn

1 English cucumber, chopped

1 bunch green onions, chopped

Juice of 1 lime

Kosher salt and freshly cracked black pepper

Microgreens for garnish (optional)

Flaky salt for finishing

Blackened Green Beans with Peanut Dipping Sauce

When I was growing up, one of my favorite restaurants our family went to was New World Home Cooking, which was right on the border of Woodstock and Saugerties. The food was so creative and exciting, and we always got the blackened green beans. New World has since closed, but I still often think about those green beans. This is my best attempt to re-create them over a campfire.

To make the dipping sauce, in a small bowl, whisk together the peanut butter, vinegar, garlic, ginger, and sugar with a fork. Season with kosher salt, then add water, a little at a time, until the mixture reaches ideal dipping consistency. Set aside.

Before you blacken the beans, I strongly recommend that you blanch them. I know it's an extra step, but it makes for a perfectly textured bean, and you can do it a day in advance. Bring a pot of salted water to a boil over high heat, drop in the beans, and boil just until they are a vibrant green, 2–4 minutes. Drain them, let them dry a little, and then coat them with a thin layer of oil. Now your beans are ready.

Light a campfire and top with a grate. When the fire is ready, place a large cast-iron frying pan on the grate and heat it until very hot. You want lots of heat to blacken the seasoning as quickly as possible so the beans remain firm. On a sheet pan, mix together the cornmeal, paprika, cumin, onion powder, kosher salt, and pepper.

When your frying pan is super hot, toss the beans in the cornmeal mixture until they are evenly and heavily coated, then immediately transfer them to the hot pan. You should hear a loud hiss and see smoke. That's a good thing. Let the beans cook until their undersides are blackened, then, using long tongs, toss them in the pan until all the cornmeal coating is blackened, 3–5 minutes.

Transfer the beans to a platter and finish with a squeeze of lime juice and a sprinkling of flaky salt. Serve immediately, with the dipping sauce.

Makes 2–4 servings

FOR THE DIPPING SAUCE

½ cup creamy peanut butter

2 tablespoons rice vinegar

1 clove garlic, grated

1-inch piece fresh ginger, peeled and grated

Pinch of sugar

Kosher salt

1 lb green beans, trimmed

Olive oil for coating the beans

2 tablespoons cornmeal

1 tablespoon smoked paprika

1 tablespoon ground cumin

1 tablespoon onion powder

Big pinch of kosher salt

1 tablespoon freshly cracked black pepper

½ lime or lemon

Flaky salt for finishing

easy sweets

Baking out in the woods is a tricky thing. Sharing baking recipes with others who are also out in the woods is even trickier. I know not everyone has an oven, and, honestly, the oven I have hardly does its job. So here's what I'll say: I've put together a collection of dessert recipes that are so far from finicky that they'll work no matter what your baking setup is. I assure you, if a toaster oven is all you have, you can still make these desserts. If a cast-iron pot or frying pan with a lid is all you have, you can still make some of these desserts. And even if you don't have access to any of those things, there are still desserts here that will work for you.

Sour Cherry and Nectarine Crisp

Is there anything better than a big, juicy midsummer fruit crisp? When this one starts to gush and bubble, the red of the cherries and the orange of the nectarines come together in a gorgeous fuchsia. It's striking. I love this served a little warm with a scoop of vanilla ice cream kinda melting over the top. The only thing that could possibly be better than that is eating a bowl of it for breakfast cold the next day. Either way, it's a beautiful way to celebrate the thick of summer. I use Morello cherries because they're the most common sour cherry and I really enjoy their brilliantly bright shade of red, but Montmorency will also work. If you can't find fresh sour cherries, you can always use frozen.

Preheat the oven to 350°F.

To make the topping, in a bowl, whisk together the flour, granulated and brown sugars, and salt. Scatter the butter over the top and, with your hands, mix everything together, thoroughly rubbing the butter pieces into the flour mixture with your fingers. The butter should be the size of peas and coated with flour. Set the topping aside.

To make the filling, in an 8 × 11-inch or similar-size baking dish, combine the nectarines, cherries, lemon zest and juice, granulated sugar, and cornstarch (if using) and gently stir and toss to mix well. Spread the filling in an even layer, then pour the topping evenly over the fruit mixture. Sprinkle the top lightly with the demerara sugar.

Bake until the top is golden and the fruit is bubbling, 1–1¼ hours. Serve warm, accompanied with ice cream if you like.

Makes about 6 servings

FOR THE TOPPING

1 cup all-purpose flour

½ cup granulated sugar

½ cup firmly packed light brown sugar

1 teaspoon kosher salt

½ cup (1 stick) cold butter, cut into small pieces

FOR THE FILLING

1½–2 lb nectarines, halved, pitted, and sliced

1 pint sour cherries (about 1 lb), pitted and halved

Grated zest and juice of 1 lemon

½ cup granulated sugar

1 teaspoon cornstarch (optional; for thickening the juices)

Demerara sugar for sprinkling

Vanilla ice cream for serving (optional)

Sweet Corn and Strawberry Jam Squares

Strawberry season is a blissful time for me. I love using the berries for jam and for baking, and sometimes they're so perfect that I just take a whole pint along with me in my truck to snack on throughout the day. I feel the same about corn. Once it's in season here in upstate New York, I eat it every way I can. In summertime, I make different versions of these delicious little squares at my pop-up, Copperhead. I've made them with raspberries, cherries, blueberries, and even wineberries I've foraged. But this is my favorite version. If strawberries aren't in season, you can make these summery bites with any jam you have on hand, but I recommend seeking out in-season strawberries that are small in size and dark in color.

Preheat the oven to 350°F. Line the bottom and sides of a 9-inch square baking pan with parchment paper.

To make the filling, in a bowl, combine the berries, lemon zest and juice, and sugar and mix with a large spoon or with your hands, mashing the berries so they become soft and jammy but keep their shape. Set the filling aside.

To make the crust, in a bowl, whisk together the all-purpose and corn flours, sugar, corn powder, and kosher salt with a fork. Add the butter and stir everything together with a spoon until a Play-Doh-like dough forms. Divide the dough in half.

Scoop half of the dough out of the bowl and press half of it onto the bottom of the parchment-lined pan, forming an even layer. Pour the strawberry mixture over the dough and, using the back of a spoon, spread it evenly over the dough. Coarsely crumble the remaining dough evenly over the strawberry mixture.

Bake until the crumble on top just starts to brown, 30–40 minutes. Remove from the oven, finish with a sprinkle of flaky salt, and let cool completely before cutting into squares.

Makes about 6 servings

FOR THE FILLING

1 pint strawberries (about ¾ lb), hulled and sliced

Grated zest and juice of 1 lemon

1–2 tablespoons sugar (depending on the sweetness of the berries)

FOR THE CRUST

2 cups all-purpose flour

1 cup corn flour

¾ cup sugar

3 tablespoons sweet corn powder

1 teaspoon kosher salt

1 cup (2 sticks) butter, melted and cooled

Flaky salt for finishing

One Bowl Lemon and Olive Oil Cake

This cake is fluffy and crispy at the same time, and I swear the recipe works best in a terrible oven. So if you're working with an ancient little oven like mine or even a toaster oven, I promise this cake will bake beautifully. You'll most likely have all these basic ingredients on hand. Just throw everything together in one bowl, pour the batter into a pan, and bake. It's super moist but crispy on the edges and is *very* lemony and bright. Make sure you're using high-quality extra-virgin olive oil. The fruitier and more floral it is, the better your little cake will be.

Preheat the oven to 350°F. Line the bottom and sides of a 9-inch round cake pan with parchment paper.

In a bowl, whisk together the flour, granulated sugar, baking soda, and salt. Add the milk, oil, butter, and lemon zest and juice and whisk until smooth. Pour the batter into the prepared pan.

Bake until the top is golden and the cake does not wobble when the pan is shaken, about 1 hour, then let cool completely. Top with berries, dust with confectioners' sugar, slice into wedges, and serve.

Makes about 8 servings

1½ cups all-purpose flour

1 cup granulated sugar

1 teaspoon baking soda

½ teaspoon kosher salt

½ cup whole milk (soy milk works too)

⅓ cup olive oil

4 tablespoons (½ stick) butter, melted and cooled

Grated zest and juice of 2 lemons

Berries (any kind) and confectioners' sugar for garnish

Little Mocha Tiramisu Cups

Tiramisu is a favorite of mine. It reminds me of dimly lit Italian restaurants that serve Chianti and really good spaghetti and meatballs—the kind of dining experience my family goes crazy for. Although I associate it with upscale dining, tiramisu is easy to put together and fares well around the campfire. Feel free to assemble these individual servings in small mason jars, glasses, nesting bowls, or mugs. Also. If you don't have a whisk, you can whip the cream to soft peaks by putting it and a clean cork into a mason jar, capping the jar tightly, and then shaking the jar vigorously.

Break the ladyfingers in half and fill 6 little dessert cups with them, 1 layer of 4 halves in each cup. In a small measuring pitcher or other vessel with a spout, stir together the coffee and rum, then pour the mixture over the ladyfingers, dividing it evenly among the cups. Set the cups aside.

In a large bowl, whisk together the cream, mascarpone, maple syrup, and vanilla until the mixture is velvety and holds soft peaks when the whisk is lifted, 3–5 minutes. Pour half of the cream mixture into a medium bowl and set aside. Add the cocoa powder to the remaining half and whisk until fully incorporated into the cream.

Divide the cocoa-cream mixture evenly among the dessert cups, spooning it on top of the coffee-soaked ladyfingers. Then do the same with the plain cream mixture. Top with the raspberries, if using, and enjoy.

Makes 6 servings

12 ladyfingers

2 cups cold brewed coffee

2 tablespoons dark rum

2 cups heavy cream

¼ cup mascarpone

2 tablespoons pure maple syrup

1 teaspoon pure vanilla extract

2 tablespoons unsweetened cocoa powder

1 pint raspberries (optional)

Blueberry Rhubarb Cobbler

Rhubarb takes my breath away. It makes anything it's added to more delicious. It's everything I'm looking for in a dessert. It's so tart it almost hurts, and I wouldn't have it any other way. I love the classic combo of strawberries and rhubarb, and you can find me eating and baking it as long as rhubarb is available at my local market. But if you're interested in wandering a little outside of the box, I think blueberries and rhubarb might be an even more delicious pairing.

Preheat the oven to 350°F.

To make the topping, in a bowl, whisk together the flour, sugar, salt, buttermilk, butter, and vanilla until smooth. Set aside.

To make the filling, in a 9-inch square baking dish, combine the blueberries, rhubarb, and sugar and gently stir and toss to mix well. Spread the filling in an even layer, then pour the topping evenly over the fruit mixture.

Bake until the top is golden and the fruit is bubbling, about 1 hour. Remove from the oven and immediately sprinkle sugar lightly over the top. Serve warm with ice cream.

Makes about 6 servings

FOR THE TOPPING

1 cup all-purpose flour

½ cup sugar, plus more for finishing

1 teaspoon kosher salt

1 cup buttermilk or whole milk

½ cup (1 stick) butter, melted and cooled

1 teaspoon pure vanilla extract

FOR THE FILLING

1 pint blueberries (about ¾ lb)

2 cups chopped rhubarb

1 cup sugar, plus more for sprinkling

Vanilla ice cream or whipped cream for serving

One Bowl Cocoa Powder Brownies

I believe these to be exceptional brownies. For me, the perfect brownie is fudgy in the middle and crispy on the outside. I want every brownie to be the corner piece, and I feel I've achieved that here. I'm also happy to report these brownies require no melting of chocolate, only cocoa powder, and they actually bake perfectly in my ancient little oven and even in a toaster oven. Be sure to cut them with a sharp knife. If they're sticky, rub a little olive oil on your knife or run it under hot water. Or, if you have a plastic knife, it should cut them with ease since it's non-stick. I hope you love them as much as I do.

Preheat the oven to 350°F. Line an 8-inch square baking pan with parchment paper.

In a bowl, whisk together the cocoa powder, flour, kosher salt, and sugars. Add the buttermilk, coconut oil, butter, and eggs and whisk until smooth. Pour the batter into the prepared pan. Sprinkle flaky salt over the top.

Bake until the top is shiny and a knife inserted into the center comes out clean, 30–40 minutes. Let cool, then cut into squares and enjoy.

Makes 12 brownies

¾ cup unsweetened cocoa powder

½ cup all-purpose flour

1 teaspoon kosher salt

1 cup granulated sugar

½ cup firmly packed light brown sugar

¼ cup buttermilk (or whatever milk you have)

¼ cup coconut oil, melted and cooled

2 tablespoons butter, melted and cooled

2 eggs, lightly beaten

Flaky salt for finishing

Lemon Curd S'mores

I don't like s'mores! I'm so sorry! They're just too much for me. The first bite is fine, but after eating one, I usually wish I hadn't. Using lemon curd instead of chocolate changes everything. Your s'more becomes a wonderful gooey bite of lemon meringue pie. The tartness of the lemon curd balances the sweetness of the marshmallow marshmallow, making for a more interesting treat.

Make these the very same way you'd make classic s'mores but top the toasted marshmallows with lemon curd instead of chocolate before placing between 2 graham crackers. An absolute delight!

Marshmallows

Lemon curd

Graham crackers

Cherry Jam and Cardamom Sticky Buns

I'm a big fan of cinnamon buns. However, they feel like a strictly cold-weather thing to me—something to cozy up with when the leaves are changing or snow is falling. Well, these buns are for any time of year. The dough is tender and the filling is sticky and juicy. I think cardamom does wonders to enhance the flavor of any fruit, and it makes the cherry jam in these absolutely sing. If you don't have a rolling pin, you can use a bottle of wine, a beer can, or even a piece of PVC pipe to roll out your dough.

To make the dough, in a small saucepan, combine the butter and milk and bring to a boil over medium heat. As soon as the mixture begins to boil, take it off the heat and let it cool until it is lukewarm (105°–115°F). Transfer the milk mixture to a large bowl and sprinkle the yeast and 1 tablespoon of the sugar over the top. Wait for about 10 minutes to allow the yeast to activate (you'll see the mixture start to bubble). Then add the flour and kosher salt and, using a large spoon, mix everything together until a rough dough forms.

Turn the dough out onto a lightly floured work surface and knead until smooth and elastic, about 5 minutes. Wash and dry the bowl and coat the inside with oil. Form the dough into a ball, place in the bowl, cover the bowl with a kitchen towel, and let the dough proof in a warm, draft-free spot until doubled in size, about 1 hour.

While the dough proofs, make the filling. In a small bowl, stir together the jam, butter, and cardamom.

When the dough is ready, line a 9-inch baking pan with parchment paper. Lightly dust the work surface again and top with the dough. Roll it out into a rectangle about 20 inches long and about ¼ inch thick. Carefully roll up the dough as tightly as you can into a log. Slice the log crosswise into 2-inch pieces, placing the pieces, cut side up, in the parchment-lined pan as they are cut. Cover the pan with the kitchen towel.

Preheat the oven to 350°F. Place the pan of buns on the stove top to proof while the oven preheats for about 20 minutes. The buns should grow noticeably in size.

Bake until golden on top, 25–30 minutes. Remove from the oven, lightly sprinkle flaky salt over the top, and enjoy.

Makes about 10 buns

FOR THE DOUGH

4 tablespoons (½ stick) butter

1 cup whole milk

1 packet of active dry yeast

2 tablespoons sugar

3 cups all-purpose flour, plus more for the work surface

1 teaspoon kosher salt

Olive oil for coating the bowl

FOR THE FILLING

½ cup cherry jam

4 tablespoons (½ stick) butter, melted and cooled

1 tablespoon ground cardamom

Flaky salt for finishing

Stone Fruit Compote

This is the laziest and most delicious dessert or breakfast option. It's fantastic on yogurt, ice cream, oatmeal, toast, shaken in a cocktail, or maybe even eaten by itself with a spoon. A jar of compote like this is always a good thing to have on hand. I call it compote because it's runnier than jam. It has a saucy kinda vibe to it, which is such a delight.

Heat a medium saucepan over medium-high heat. Add the fruit and let it soften and bubble down for about 10 minutes. Add ½ cup of the sugar and stir with a large spoon. Continue to cook, stirring often and tasting and adding more sugar as needed, until the fruit breaks down and thickens, about 20 minutes.

When most of the fruit has broken down, stir in the lemon zest and juice and continue to cook, stirring often, until the mixture is thick enough to lightly coat the spoon, about 5 minutes longer. Remove from the heat and let cool completely. Spoon into glass jars, cap tightly, and store in your cooler or fridge.

Makes about two 8-oz jars

2 lb stone fruit, such as peaches, nectarines, cherries, apricots, or a mix of whatever you can find

½–1 cup sugar (depending on the sweetness of the fruit)

Grated zest and juice of 1 lemon

Apple Tart with Brown Butter Crust

This sweet and tender little tart is the perfect recipe when apples are in season. The brown butter crust is crumbly and crispy like a shortbread cookie. I love to use Gala or Honeycrisp apples because they're bright and tart, and I love using raw honey because it's creamy and lovely. Both the filling and the crust come together easily.

Preheat the oven to 350°F. Line the bottom and sides of a 9-inch pie pan with parchment paper.

To make the crust, in a small saucepan, melt the butter over medium-high heat and allow to cook, swirling the pan often, until the butter browns and smells like caramel, 5–8 minutes. Remove from the heat.

In a bowl, whisk together the flour, brown sugar, and kosher salt. Add the butter and stir until well mixed and a rough dough forms. (It should be the consistency of sandy Play-Doh.) Wrap the dough in parchment paper and place it in the fridge or cooler while you make the filling.

To make the filling, in a large bowl, combine the apples, honey, kosher salt, lemon zest and juice, and cornstarch and stir and toss to mix well.

Transfer the dough to the prepared pie pan and press it evenly over the bottom and up the sides. With your fingers, shape the top edge of the dough into an even ring, then gently flute the ring by pressing it between the thumb of one hand and the index finger and thumb of the other. Pour the apple filling into the dough-lined pan and spread it evenly. Lightly sprinkle the top with demerara sugar and flaky salt.

Bake until the apples are tender and the crust has become a slightly deeper brown, 45–60 minutes. Let cool completely, then cut into slices and serve with ice cream.

Makes 6–8 servings

FOR THE CRUST

1 cup (2 sticks) butter

3 cups all-purpose flour

½ cup firmly packed light brown sugar

1 teaspoon kosher salt

FOR THE FILLING

4 Gala or Honeycrisp apples (about 1 lb), halved, cored, and sliced paper-thin

⅓ cup raw honey

1 teaspoon kosher salt

Grated zest and juice of 1 lemon

1 tablespoon cornstarch

Demerara sugar and flaky salt for finishing

Vanilla ice cream or whipped cream for serving

index

ACKNOWLEDGMENTS

SPECIAL THANKS TO: My wonderful agent Adriana for all that you do. Your encouragement and guidance has been invaluable. My editor Amy for believing in my story, and designer Chrissy for truly understanding my vision. The incredible Danielle and both of my brothers for such thorough recipe testing help. Sean's parents, Laura and Marko, for all the support through this weird and wild chapter of our lives. Story Farms, MX Morning Star Farms, Davenport Farms and Adams Faire Acre Farms for growing and offering the most beautiful ingredients a cook could ask for. John for the unwavering support and optimism. For all the taste testing, beers, and fires. For being a constant reminder that life is something to be enjoyed and friendship is something to celebrate. Brittany: For truly everything. Thank you for bringing our dream to life and for understanding me beyond words. The best part of this experience was having you by my side. I'm so grateful. To the Hudson Valley and the Catskill Mountains for being my lifelong muse. And to my beloved community here. You are my home. Forever.

weldon**owen**

an imprint of Insight Editions
PO Box 3088
San Rafael, CA 94912
www.weldonowen.com

ISBN: 979-8-88674-078-3

Manufactured in China by Insight Editions
10 9 8 7 6 5 4 3 2 1

The information in this book is provided as a resource for inspiration and education. Author and Publisher expressly disclaim any responsibility for any adverse effects from the use or application of the information contained in this book. Neither the Publisher nor Author shall be liable for any losses suffered by any reader of this book.

Weldon Owen would also like to thank Rachel Markowitz, Elizabeth Parson, and Sharon Silva for copyediting, for proofreading, and for indexing.

CEO: Raoul Goff
VP Publisher: Roger Shaw
Associate Publisher: Amy Marr
Publishing Director: Katie Killebrew
VP Creative: Chrissy Kwasnik
VP Manufacturing: Alix Nicholaeff
Sr Production Manager: Joshua Smith
Sr Production Manager, Subsidiary Rights:
    Lina s Palma-Temena

Photographer: Brittany Barb

Insight Editions, in association with Roots of Peace, will plant two trees for each tree used in the manufacturing of this book. Roots of Peace is an internationally renowned humanitarian organization dedicated to eradicating land mines worldwide and converting war-torn lands into productive farms and wildlife habitats. Roots of Peace will plant two million fruit and nut trees in Afghanistan and provide farmers there with the skills and support necessary for sustainable land use.